They Said She Couldn't

So She Did

Kendra Blevins Ford

Copyright 2019

This book is a biographical work based on the actual audio recordings that Bernice D. Smith Blevins Tongate created in the late 1980s, which have been transcribed by this author simply by listening and without the use of any transcription software.

No portion of this book shall be copied or used without permission.

Kendra Blevins Ford

The author owns all photographs within this book.

Front cover design: Kendra Blevins Ford

Interior Design: Michelle Morrow www.chellreads.com

Signed Navy poster (public domain) on front cover and within text, owned by the author.

It always seems impossible until it's done.

-*Nelson Mandela*

DEDICATION

This work is dedicated to the memory of my great-grandmother, Bernice D. Smith Blevins Tongate. May she live on in both our hearts and American history for the important part she had in both.

I would also like to dedicate this book to my husband, Chris, my sons Jake and Cody, as well as my father and mother, Paul and Kathy Blevins, who carefully kept Grandma's audiotapes in safekeeping all these years.

Table of Contents

Copyright 2019

DEDICATION

Prologue

Introduction

Chapter 1 Who Have We Got? 1

Chapter 2 The Best-Kept Secret 19

Chapter 3 San Fernando Valley 22

Chapter 4 Valle Vista 27

Chapter 5 Harvest Time 42

Chapter 6 Missions 52

Chapter 7 Rae Lake 57

Chapter 8 What Do I Do Now? 73

Chapter 9 Navy Wife 95

Chapter 10 Leucadia 117

Chapter 11 Prescott 127

Chapter 12 Los Angeles 134

Chapter 13 Burbank, California 144

Chapter 14 Redding, California 152

Chapter 15 Bay Area 163

Chapter 16 Alaska 173

Chapter 17 Seattle 195

Chapter 18 Sequim 209

Chapter 19 Shelton 223

Chapter 20 Washington Veterans Home 230

Acknowledgements 240

For Further Reading 241

Prologue

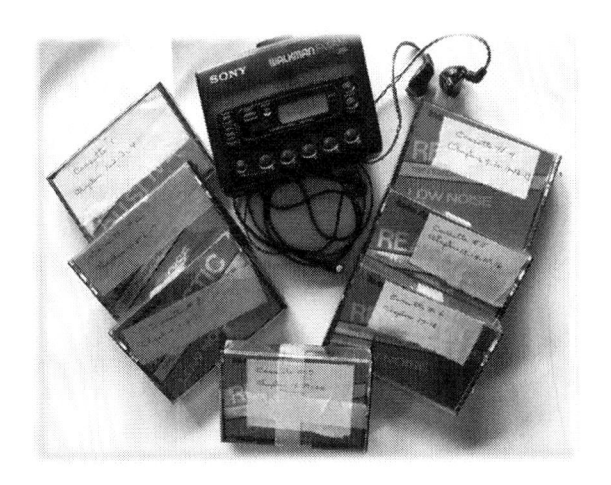

My great-grandmother on my father's side, Bernice D. Smith Blevins Tongate, recorded the most memorable events of her life on cassette tapes during her last several years on earth, while in a hospital bed; I believe the year they were finished was 1984. These cassette tapes were mailed to our home in Illinois all the way from Washington state. At the time we received this priceless gift of hers, I was about 12 years old. I never took the time to listen to her story when I was a child. Now that I am in my late 40s, I have finally listened to her amazing life story and marvel at her courage, grit, and strength. I will admit that the transcription process was slow. I painstakingly typed out every word at first, rewinding and re-playing a Sony Walkman to ensure I got the details down correctly. Numerous times during the arduous transcription process, she was quite difficult to hear. I used high-quality

hearing equipment to help diffuse the background hum and static that was characteristic of cassette tape recordings from that era.

This book is about my Great-Grandma Bernice's life, stated in her words, her way. As one may note, not all parts of her life are provided in detail. She tends to provide excellent detail in some life reflections, yet barely mentions others. This makes me pause . . . and leaves me wondering why. While listening, I felt that she wanted to tell her story years ago but lacked resources and appropriate connections to do so. Remarkably, she describes in one of the chapters how she attended a writing class in order to learn how to write her autobiography. Unfortunately, her deteriorating health not only dictated her path, but also her choice of home, as well as her daily activities late in life.

While writing her biography, I preserved the words of her story as much as possible but have edited for clarity and readability. All chapter titles are Bernice's own. Some of her thoughts on life may be offensive to some according to today's political correctness, as they sometimes relate to "the olden days and how things used to be." These thoughts are solely hers and were left in the book as it was a part of who she was at the time of her recordings and how she viewed life. She does have a strong opinion on some topics. Remember, she was born in 1897 and lived for 92 years so she has seen, heard, and experienced things we have only read of in books. Through the transcription process, I have verified spellings, locations, and dates as much as possible to preserve the authenticity of her story. Some names of people or locations simply cannot be retraced or located, so they may not be spelled correctly and will need to be viewed as placeholders of sorts so as to not interrupt the flow of her dialogue.

While listening to her voice on the audiocassette tapes, I discovered many things that we share in common. The curly brown hair of my youth is certainly one, but I also love flower, fruit, and vegetable gardening. I've always had a knack for artistry and crafting, interests we also share. We have so many more similarities, which others can discover as they continue reading. If anyone wonders where my spunk and spirit comes from, I believe that would be from my Great-Grandmother Bernice. I also believe that, someday when we are united in Heaven, we will have much to talk about.

Well, it's time to tell Bernice's story. I have gladly taken the baton and am proud to be called the first great-granddaughter of Bernice Smith Blevins Tongate: the woman who was told she couldn't . . . so she did.

Introduction

Bernice begins her story with family genealogy. While this may be as interesting as reading a passage in Leviticus to some, to me, it is a treasured report of who my ancestors were. This genealogical revelation was checked for accuracy via www.ancestry.com. The process of looking up documents and determining fact from lore was quite fulfilling to me. Don't worry, this chapter is also sprinkled with interesting tidbits of wagon train tales and such, so historical buffs may find this chapter most interesting. My great-grandmother Bernice begins her recordings by saying,

"I want to introduce you to the members of the family you have never known. This has been the most interesting and amazing age to have lived in! Here are a few examples of the changes during the twentieth century: electricity, telephones, washers and dryers, radio, TV, paved sidewalks and roads, modern plumbing, elevators, escalators, planes, men walking on the moon, as well as hearing their voices from the moon, and so much more! So, remember the amazing age . . . and forget my age, ha ha! This is my gift to you. A sample of modern means of communication; a set of talking books you might save."

Chapter 1

Who Have We Got?

To the best of my knowledge and belief, this is an accurate record of all the additions and subtractions as told to me by my parents and grandparents. To begin, I will tell you about my mother's side of the family. My grandmother on my mother's side was Althea Delia Trask. She married Edward Payson Fish. They had one living child, Emma May Fish (two other children were also born but died during their first year).

My grandma claimed with *great* pride that she was related to a passenger on the Mayflower, who was the first governor of Virginia, namely, Governor Winthrop. Grandpa and Daddy were always quick to remind everyone that none of their families had "fled their country," but were born in the good ol' U.S.A. Apparently, this was a family jest that came up from time to time.

Grandma and her sister had referenced a search of the family heritage. And it was reported to be true that Cousin Herbert knew how to go about and obtain a photo of the family coat of arms. I was also informed that my mother crocheted a doily of it. I believe it was given to my sister, Lucile. She may have given it to one of her sons, but the location of it is unknown as of this writing. As near as I can figure it out, my grandpa, Edward Payson Fish, must have been born about 1842. *[Ancestry.com believes it was actually 1832 according to many sources.]* He was a Confederate soldier who joined the army at the age of 19.

I believe my grandparents lived near Princeton, Illinois. When Mama was just 5 years old, all of them decided to go west. Uncles, aunts, cousins, and some of their good neighbors, all came by covered wagon to Colorado from Illinois.

I want to interject here and add an anecdote. When my mother was recovering from the birth of Damaris, my baby sister, Grandpa used to go to the hospital to visit her and tell her about their trip across the plains. Mama wrote down the details of these stories, but it was lost some time ago.

My grandma was a school teacher before she was married. She related many stories of the wagon trains of yesteryear. In one telling, she described the story of how during a wagon train stop, she gathered all of the children around her and taught them "the three Rs: reading, writing, and arithmetic." In another of these stories, she also informed me that they had to kill several of their own horses because they had eaten "locoweed" during the journey; apparently it made them quite vicious. I once asked someone if that could have been marijuana that the horses ate, and the answer provided was that "it undoubtedly was."

My grandma's brother, A. Chandler Trask, made handles for kitchen forks and spoons out of buffalo ribs so they might have utensils for eating during the covered wagon journey. I once had a cooking spoon and a fork that he created, but it has since disappeared.

Another story I will never forget is when they had to deal with [Native Americans] two or three times during the journey to Colorado. On one particular day, my family's wagon train came upon the smoking remains of another wagon train. Our folks always sent scouts ahead of them to avoid ambush. On one occasion, the scouts returned and told everyone to wrap gunnysacks around the wheels, as well as around the feet of all the animals. They also had to tie something around the children's mouths, as well as the dogs, to avoid any noise. They had seen [Native Americans] in war paint and wanted to detour around them if they could! This precaution was both wise *and* successful.

They Said She Couldn't So She Did

Another unfortunate time on the wagon train was when the water containers on some of the wagons leaked; they were out of water for quite a while. To help the children cope with the lack of water, the women strung large buttons on cords like a necklace and told the children to put the large button in their mouth and suck on it. The children soon learned that by doing so, they would not get quite as thirsty as their mouths would not get so dry.

Contrary to assumptions about what happened years ago regarding covered wagon trains and [Native American] encounters, our people did not have any trouble with them. In fact, our people traded bright fabric material, beads, and buttons for baskets, pottery, blankets, moccasins, and even a few bow and arrow sets. Mama used to go to our schools and tell about this trip, and show these unique, historical items, but little by little, all of these things have unfortunately vanished. We thought we knew who had taken them, but not having seen the missing items, we couldn't prove their location or existence.

When Grandpa told us about these adventures, neither Lucile nor I could ask questions; children were to be "seen and not heard." This was impressed upon the backside of our lap in a most tortuous way.

Kendra Blevins Ford

The only historical thing left from this time period (to my knowledge) is a watercolor picture, a New England picture to be exact, and a cornmeal table made of woven grass. These items were reportedly used in ceremonial dances. The location of these items is currently unknown, however.

Now back to the family tree: Emma Chloe Trask was my grandmother's sister; she married Emery Kays. They had two sons: Herbert and Arnold, and a daughter, Lucile. The sons graduated from New York Academy. Both were captains in World War I. After their parent's death, we lost track of them and also their sister, after she married.

Chandler Trask was Grandma's brother. He and his wife had one child: Tallman Trask. He lived in Pasadena, California, and was very active in the Masonic lodge. Unfortunately, not a single one of my mailed letters to them have been returned to me, nor answered. Tallman had one son, Tallman Jr., but I have not heard from him, either.

They Said She Couldn't So She Did

My dear mother *(pictured above)* was a graduate of Agnes Conservatory of Music in Decatur, Georgia. That is where she met my father, Graham Smith. When she completed her musical education, she returned to Pueblo, Colorado. They apparently kept their relationship going via mailed letters, and one day Graham Smith wrote to my mother and said he would like to come out for a visit to see her and meet her parents. The evening before he was due to arrive, it rained heavily and there was a large puddle in the front yard. Grandpa was a bit of a jokester and put up a sign: "No Fishing!" But that didn't bother Daddy nor deter him from seeing my mother and meeting her parents.

Regretfully, I do not know much about my father's side of the family. I do know that his mother was Euphrasia Damaris Raggs. She married Sully Smith, and they had three sons: Henry, Duncan, and Graham. I believe Henry and Duncan were killed in the Spanish-American War. My daddy's parents died when the boys were very young.

Aunt Carrie, sister of Grandma Damaris, took her three boys to Wales. Aunt Carrie Blaine also had a daughter, named Megan, who stayed in America and married Paul Hamilton, whose family lived on a huge tobacco plantation in Kentucky. When President Abraham Lincoln freed the slaves, Uncle Paul gave each one of the slaves a plot of land and their freedom, but everyone stayed on and worked for Uncle Paul. I do not know whether the old ones left on the plantation were the slaves or the actual Hamilton kinfolk.

They Said She Couldn't So She Did

I believe I am the only one of Daddy's children to have gone back to the old home in August, Kentucky. Uncle Paul had died prior to my visit, but old Charlotte, who helped raise my daddy, as well as his brothers, was still there. I'll never forget her appearance when I first met her. She was an *enormous* woman, with snow-white hair, and a heart of gold. She used to call my daddy, "Grio." She hugged me, laughing and crying, all at the same time, saying, "Grio's little girl and his grandson has come home!" She must have been about 95 years old, much too old to work, but you can be sure she kept the house spic and span as she always had. Believe me: there was no slovenliness, no slouching workers around as long as she was the boss.

Oh, but there was a delight for me during my visit that I must mention: homemade ice cream! Charlotte brought me a large, old-fashioned soup bowl full of ice cream. "That's what your daddy always wanted," she said. I ate every bit of it.

Now, Uncle Paul went to law school in Covington, Kentucky. He graduated and practiced law for a while, but he could not earn an honest living to support his family because he would not (or could not) defend a man guilty of a crime. His reasoning was this: "If you stay within the law, you won't need a lawyer." I don't know what he would say if he could see the way lots of legal professions contribute to lawlessness today. He decided to walk away from practicing law and have a career change. He took up home and fire insurance, and I guess you would call him an insurance broker. He had posters for Prudential and Mutual of Omaha, as well as different fire insurance posters, displayed in his office.

My dear Daddy (*pictured above*), Graham Smith, was tall and slender and wore a mustache with a beard that he kept neatly trimmed. A fine, distinguished gentleman, he had a fine sense of humor but was also fair and square about everything. He believed that there are two sides to everything: right and wrong, obedient and disobedient, lawful or unlawful. He never took advantage of *anyone* just to get the biggest part.

My oldest sister and best friend, Lucile, was born in Pueblo, Colorado, on August 31, 1894. (*Many documents and photos in this writer's possession have Lucile's name spelled with only one "l" contrary to traditional spelling.*) I was born there also, on December 14, 1897. I was very young when my folks came out to California. We have lived all over the state of California, from up north in Black Bear to the south part of the state in San Diego. You name it, we lived there.

After we had lived in northern California for a while, Grandma and Grandpa came up from Colorado. The move to California was particularly hard on Grandpa. He would go downtown, come home, and say, "I'd give a lot just to hear a familiar voice say, 'Hello, Red! How are ya?'" Although Grandpa was not very happy with the move to California, Grandma was very happy here. She was with her "little girl" (my mother)!

I want to tell you about an interesting event that happened when I was very young, 8 or 9 years old I believe. One morning, as we were having breakfast, our gold overhead lamp (which hung from the ceiling and could be pulled up and down on a chain) suddenly began to swing. Daddy told Mama to grab it, but I was quicker and reached it first, and did the opposite. I lowered it. All of a sudden, dishes began to skid on the table, and a window broke in the kitchen. Some of the dishes fell out of the cupboard. I remember there being strange rumbling sounds, and that we felt kind of sick. Well, I later learned that we had experienced the San Francisco earthquake that struck in 1906—and we were 500 miles away! It is hard to fathom what it would have felt like if we had been any closer.

When I was very young, our family built a lovely home (*pictured above*) in Hollywood in the Van Nuys annex; it was just north of Franklin, at the foot of Mt. Hollywood, and west of the Sacred Heart Convent. Damaris Althea Smith, my baby sister, was born soon after we moved in there on May 3, 1907. A year after this, our doctor informed my parents that I wouldn't live much longer. I had always been a sickly child and had come down with pneumonia seven times. Well, they were wrong, because as you will continue to see, I lived many decades. The doctor also said that Daddy could only live a couple more years; this was in 1908. But, truth be told, my daddy lived until 1915!

I fondly recall in my younger years that I always wanted Daddy to sit and hold my hands until I fell asleep. He went downtown one day and it was very hot. The weather must have done something to him or affected his breathing negatively. Well, he came home that day and promptly laid down for a nap. He didn't come up out of his bed, though. Unfortunately, he took pleurisy and died two days later, on September 30, 1915. This was a turn of events that I was not expecting. It was my turn now; I was the one who sat by *his* bed and held *his* hands until he went to sleep, only he didn't wake up. He was beloved and dearly missed by many. I miss his wise ways as well as his extraordinary gift of understanding children most of all.

On the subject of friends, I want to tell an interesting story involving my parents and some of their good friends. Back then it was common for us to entertain friends on a regular basis, and we usually had someone over on a Sunday. On one particular

They Said She Couldn't So She Did

Sunday, we had a Dr. Nicholson and his wife over. They brought an elderly couple along with them to visit with Grandpa and Grandma, thinking they might have something in common. Well, they had something in common all right. We were all having a fine time until the women left to set up the buffet table for cake, coffee, and ice cream. The two oldest men were swapping tales about their Civil War experiences. Grandpa was telling him of a battle at such and such a place, and said, "Some damn Yankee up in that church property began shooting at me. He couldn't hit the side of a barn!" He was jumping up and down like all get out. The other older man suddenly jumped up and yelled at Grandpa, "Well, you damn Rebel, you must have had lice or fleas in your pants the way you were jumping around." To this, my Grandpa retorted, "Well, why don't we finish up the unfinished business, shall we?" Dr. Nicholson felt the need to intervene and said to them, "You two old roosters better calm down now; the war is all over, we are all good Americans and good neighbors, and you better just shake hands all around, doggone it!" By that time, cake, coffee, and ice cream were ready to be enjoyed, all disagreements had been settled, and so we all took part and ate cake.

Not long after that, my grandpa became bedridden, which was incredibly difficult for all of us. I remember how he used to love having a baby tucked in bed beside him. He had a long, snow-white beard, the likes of which no Santa Claus could equal. Poor old dear, with ten baby fingers all tangled up in his beard, there would be tears streaming down his face until someone noticed and came to Grandpa's rescue. He died in our home on October 1, 1907. I'm sure it was just home lonesomeness that caused him to pass. I don't recall him being ill at the time he became bedridden; he seemed to have simply given up on life.

Unfortunately, Grandma failed rapidly in health after Grandpa died. I believe she was in her seventies when she passed in August of 1916. On this somber subject, my dear mother died on Easter Sunday while residing in Brookings, Oregon. I never did know much about the events surrounding her death, since I was over in Prescott, Arizona, at the time and was dealing with depression. I believe that was 1931, or it might have been 1933.

My sister Lucile graduated from Occidental College with a teaching degree. As she would have had to attend two *additional* years of college in order to teach in California, she decided to go to Tempe, Arizona, and secure a teaching position there instead. This was during World War I. You bet your last dollar *none* of her school kids ever said, "ain't no use no how." She was very particular in teaching the children how to speak correctly and respectfully.

Lucile renewed her friendship with Warren Payne and married him July 7, 1920. William B., their first child, made a name for himself during WWII. He is known to have retired from the army as a major. Warren W. Payne, their second son, graduated from Yale with honors and was a legal advisor for a steel ship company for a number of years. William B. and Jean, his wife, had three sons: Larry, Chuck, and Doug. They lived in Vancouver, Washington. Larry was up in Alaska for a long time, somewhere near Turtle Bay.

Lucile returned to California after teaching in Arizona, where she and Warren bought a fine home in San Rafael. Her last home was a lovely one they purchased in Napa. None of us had any idea Lucile was having heart trouble. I doubt that she even knew her heart was going to give out, but it did. She died December 26, 1969. Her sudden death was extremely shocking and awful to me. I used to hear her voice every day. And then suddenly it hits you, and you know you'll never hear it again. It does something to you.

Kendra Blevins Ford

You will note throughout Bernice's story how dear her sister Lucile was to her. Truly, they had a kinship that only sisters can fully understand. Although it may seem repetitive, the very fact that Bernice mentions Lucile frequently in her life story is a testament to the love and devotion she had for her older sister.

I married Harrison (Harry) Halsted Blevins on July 7, 1920. Harry and I had two sons: Graham H. Blevins was born March 28, 1922, and my second son, Christopher Blevins, who died at birth, in 1924. Unfortunately, Harry and I were divorced when Graham was only 7 years old. Graham joined the Marines during World War II and was stationed in the South Pacific, on Cape Gloucester. He was an avid photographer; he brought home some amazing pictures of the bombing in Japan. He came home from the war, thank goodness, safe and sound. He married Virginia H. Lalowski, and they had three children: Paul, James, and Helene. Their marriage was not successful, either, unfortunately. Paul joined the Navy and served in the Pacific during Vietnam. Paul has two fine children, Kendra and Ian. Kendra was my very first great-grandchild, and Ian was my second. James was in the army and also served in Vietnam. And both grandsons came home, thank God, safe and sound. James had one son named Douglas. Helene lived in California but has never married. She was an inhalation therapist and put herself

They Said She Couldn't So She Did

through training, which is no small job, believe me. Graham married again, this time to Donaldine, and she had a daughter Cindy, and a son, Rob. There, my dears, are the family.

Chapter 2

The Best-Kept Secret

My family and I moved to California in 1898. My papa's business took him to so many places in California, which caused us to move frequently; we lived in many different parts of the state during my growing up years. Grandma and Grandpa came out to visit us when we lived in Oakland.

One of my dearest memories of my childhood, while we lived in Oakland, was when my grandpa would take my sister Lucile and me over to San Francisco on the ferry, which was then followed by a trip to Golden Gate Park. This excursion occurred about once a week. There was a fenced-in area where they had Shetland ponies; they were attached to little carts where children could ride as passengers in the carts and imagine they were just like the grown-ups. After the pony cart ride, we would go over toward the Japanese Tea Garden. There was something very special to us there: a tunnel. A tunnel may seem like an ordinary thing, but to us it was magical. Grandpa would tell one of us to go to the opposite end while the other one remained where he was. Grandpa would say, "Now, when I wave my magic wand, be sure to yell, just as loud as you can, and start running toward each other. Do this until I blow my whistle." This was just wonderful to us because, during this time, no one said, "Shush, you're too noisy. Be quiet." We called this our magic tunnel. From there, we went to the marvelous merry-go-round, and oh what fun that was. After this, we had a priceless treat: one tiny cup of tea for two and two fortune cookies, one for each of us. I often wondered if Mama ever knew or suspected that we had that forbidden tea. I doubt it. I bet you it was the best-kept secret in the world, especially to Lucile and me. This was about 1900.

Fast forward to 1965, when I visited Lucile who lived in San Rafael, just across the Golden Gate Bridge from San Francisco. She suggested we go through the museum. We drove over and found a good parking place and started to walk over toward the tallest building we saw. The sidewalk curled around some shrubbery. Lucile said, "Look! That's our old magic tunnel." As if on cue, both of us let out an ear-splitting "hello." The magic still worked. For, sure enough, we heard "hello" as an echo. Lucile said it was as loud as when Grandpa had told her to yell as a youngster. Wouldn't he have laughed at his two grown-up grandchildren reliving a fond memory! Just then, I

Kendra Blevins Ford

looked down at the end of the tunnel, and there was an old, white-haired gentleman, leaning on his cane. He was laughing as hard as he could while still remain standing, as two old, white-haired women relived a precious moment of their childhood. I have often wondered who that gentleman really was that day.

Chapter 3

San Fernando Valley

Bernice as a young girl, early 1900s

Kendra Blevins Ford

Shortly after my grandparents visited us in Oakland, they came out to California to live permanently. Two things I fondly recall about my grandparents include Grandma being a wonderful cook and Grandpa being the most understanding person. No child could have had more of it. I could do lots of things while growing up, but it made me mad if only boys could do certain things like climb trees or play marbles, which was "not a ladylike thing to do." Sometimes I think it was a mistake for the [grandparents] to move out to California permanently. I wonder if they were "too old to be transplanted." Grandma and Grandpa were comfortable and happy, but there was an unavoidable generation gap, even in those days. I believe there will be, and always will be, a generation gap. Why? Because as children, you are not old enough to do so and so or to know about this or that. Then, when you reach the "inconvenient age," we are told, "You cannot do that anymore. Take it easy." This is the generation gap we realize even today, and it is unavoidable.

A couple of years after my grandparents moved near us, our old family doctor informed us that Daddy would have to give up his business and get out into the country where the air was fresh and clean. We made an arrangement to have a woman come and stay with Grandma from early Friday afternoon until late Sunday afternoon. Papa and Mama would drive over to our school and give us some overalls and an old blouse to put on, as well as old shoes. We would go to the locker room of the school gym and change in a hurry to get started on another adventurous weekend. The surrey was always packed with camping gear and plenty of food for us, and harnessed to our white horse. We drove out over the clinking paths of Hollywood to San Fernando Valley.

We took an enormous hard-bound dictionary with us on this trip so that I could press the numerous specimens of wildflowers (as many as I could find) between its pages. This really paid off nicely. The Hollywood women's club was going to have a flower show and offer fine prizes for the largest collection of wildflowers and a prize for the best, as well as the rarest, wildflowers. To my surprise, I won both first prizes! One prize was a lovely book: California Wildflowers by Ann. S. Davidson. Sadly, it's out of print now. The other prize was a lovely picture by Paul Delondry, a famous California artist at the time. Unfortunately, both prizes were destroyed by moisture and mold when they were inadvertently left in a storage trunk.

On our first weekend camping trip, we didn't find anything that appealed to my folks as a satisfactory place to move to. We kept wondering what the north side of the valley might be like, at least sure that it would not be flat or have a view of anything, so we went over to that side. It was getting late in the afternoon. We found a nice-looking place to camp. The place was within easy walking distance to a farmhouse to buy fresh milk. It had a dry river bed, so no danger if we build a campfire. Daddy unloaded the surrey, Mama started supper, Lucile made up the beds, and I gathered sage twigs for the fire. Daddy had turned his back and was just getting ready to eat when Mama let out a terrifying scream. There was just a little bit of water coming down the dry stream bed, but she was afraid it was going to be like some of those "Colorado freshers," or flash flood. We must have set a world record for speed, breaking up camp and moving it up the bank. I do not think the riverbed was any deeper, or as deep, as a bathtub. Later past supper, at family prayers, Mama reminded the Lord that we trusted Him to hold the water back as He did for the children of Israel. The water seemed to get just so high, and no higher. While mama was carrying out breakfast, we noticed that the water was going down. We didn't even have time to fill up the canteen! We found out that our wonderful supply of fresh water was not such a strange thing after all. The hired man at the ranch where we had gotten fresh milk had been irrigating his orange grove. At quitting time, they closed the floodgates and turned the water down the old dry river bed. I

They Said She Couldn't So She Did

think the good Lord must have had quite a little chuckle over this.

We went to the town of San Fernando and talked with a real estate agent. He informed us of several places, but none of them looked quite right. We decided to come back directly to this area next week and study it more thoroughly.

Chapter 4

Valle Vista

In Bernice's recordings, she pronounces her beloved childhood ranch home as "VY-A" Vista. It wasn't until I saw the incredible vintage photographs of her childhood home of Valle Vista and noted the correct spelling that I made the necessary changes in order to preserve the factual spelling and references she includes in this chapter. I have a love of land, trees, and open spaces. Another trait that my great-grandmother and I share. Her childhood home sounds like an amazing place to live full of adventure, promise, and hard work- something that never intimidated either of us. The picture that follows is from Bernice's mother's scrapbook. The inscription says "Our Live Stock."

They Said She Couldn't So She Did

The very next week we went directly to the real estate agent, and sure enough, he had a different place for us to go see. It was a section of land, with 640 acres, that no one had lived on for several years, except squatters, who just camped there. If we decided to buy it, he promised to have these people vacated and the area cleaned up.

We were quite taken with the beautiful view of the entire valley as well as the peace and quiet. We were captivated by the plaintive coo of wild doves and the unfamiliar sound of a covey of quail in flight. There was a small stream, (ha ha, not one you turn off and on), and the Hollywood hills could be seen in the distance, clear across the valley. The valley was full of green fields as far as one could see. Close to us were orange groves, as well as the largest olive grove in the world at that time. There was an enormous barn with a hayloft, which neither Lucile nor I had ever seen before. The property had plentiful spaces for sacks of grain, flocks of chickens, storage for pumpkins, and a section for hanging up the horse tack and harness. Across from this was a long low building made of adobe bricks and a tile roof. That building had three sections to it: one for chickens with roosts and nests, the second one without any doors and large enough for a hay wagon, surrey, and farm equipment. Then there was the third and largest room for the farm animals. There was also a bunkhouse at one end of this building with a very unusual fireplace in the corner of the room. We had never seen one like it before. It was not on the floor, but rather on a slightly raised adobe brick platform. This, I imagine, was a welcome adjustment, as one did not have to bend over all the time to cook from this setup. The most unique feature of this cooking setup was a hammered-rock iron arm that could be swung over the fire as well as swung out. It had three hooks on it so you could cook several things at one time.

We walked up to the canyon a short distance ahead and found a delightful place to camp over the weekend. In fact, by this point, we were just about sold on the place. If this lovely camping spot we had just come upon happened to be on the land we were thinking of buying, this spot definitely decided the matter for us.

Daddy began to measure off space for the location of flooring for various sized tents that we would use until we could build our house. We had to have a place to keep clothing, places to arrange furniture, a food pantry safe from predators, clean linen for sleeping, as well as books and personal things in their own special places—all the while keeping everything clean and dry while maintaining appropriate sleeping quarters for every member of the family. The house the squatters had inhabited could not be made clean enough for us to live in. The squatters apparently had tamed and trained a family of skunks to come get bread to eat from them. Our family would not be doing the same!

The gorgeous view of the valley helped in our decision to name our new property Valle Vista Valley View. There would be a broad space for Grandma's tent, which could accommodate her bed, chiffonier, trunk, and her beloved rocker, plus a space to hang up her clothing. Then a larger broad space for Mama and Daddy, for their bed and personal belongings. A third and enormous tent was for us to use as a kitchen, dining room, living room, and kids' study area. When Daddy had this all measured and sketched out, we drove into town to see what kind of schools and churches existed and what the neighborhood looked like. Everything "passed inspection" with flying colors according to Daddy.

Our family went over to the real estate agent and informed him that we wanted to buy the property. We also gave him the plans for our camping needs. He said he would get a good word out regarding our need of a foreman to help run the ranch and barn. He wanted to know the exact date that we would move on to the property so he could have this man there to help unload and place our furniture where we wanted it. Everything moved like clockwork. And true to his word, the real estate agent ensured our much-needed foreman was there for us on that Friday.

Our new foreman's name was Salidonia Rodriguez. He was of Mexican descent and was not fluent in English. Our family did not speak Spanish, so Daddy bought each member of the family an English-Spanish vest-pocket-sized dictionary to help us learn to communicate with Salidonia. We could look the word up we needed and attempt to say it, and "Honde Sali," as we called him, laughed and tried to teach us. This amused Sali so he cut out pictures of a cat, dog, cow, chicken, and horse, pasted them on paper, and made a dictionary for Damaris, who was just a toddler at the time. He would point to a cat and go, "Meow," and then say "cat" in Spanish. The same scenario ensued with all of the animals that needed a Spanish translation. When Damaris said the word "horse" in her Spanish baby-talk style, he would get down on his hands and knees and offer her a piggyback ride on his big broad back. He just adored the baby. He was also thoughtful, kind, and considerate to Grandma. Even she admitted that Salidonia was nice. When Grandma wandered away from the tent, old Sali suddenly appeared from nowhere, stepped in front of Grandma, took off his sombrero, swept it around her, and then gently steered her back to her rocking chair.

On weekends, when we were not working, we would go for a walk: inspecting (and gloating) over our wonderful, expansive ranch. On one occasion, we walked up to the canyon beyond our campsite and observed that the hills were covered with huge holly trees with clusters of green holly berries all over them. Daddy had an idea. He sent my older sister Lucile back to camp to get all of the old rags or worn-out sheets Mama could spare. He then tied pieces of these rags onto the trees that had the best berries. Soon we ran out of rags, so we just walked on up to the canyon to see what else we might discover.

When we passed a certain point, we realized that we were in the forest reserve, which meant this was government property, and that no one could build on the back of our property. By this point, we had walked about a mile up the canyon and found that the main stream was getting closer. Soon there was no place left to walk except *in* the stream, so we took off our shoes and stockings and tied them to a tree. When we had waded just around the bend, we were astonished to see a gorgeous waterfall! The granite walls around the waterfall came close together at the top. I do not think the sun ever shone there, except at high noon.

The sides of the waterfall were covered with lovely maidenhair fern. We were inspired to discover what could be beyond that beautiful waterfall.

When we returned to the place where we'd hung up our shoes, we sat down to rest our feet for a while. Daddy had an idea, and as was his custom, he was busy sketching his idea out on paper. When he had finished his sketch, he showed us his drawing. He had drawn a drag sled complete with a horse dragging it. As soon as we returned to our camp, he sat down and made a better drawing, then gave it to Salidonia. He implored Salidonia to create a drag sled similar to his drawing, as well as a very long ladder (in those days we built things we needed if we could, rather than buy them in a store). Our good and faithful Salidonia made the drag sled with old scrap iron runners on it. He also created a tall ladder for us. When he was finished, we had a holiday of sorts, and we told Salidonia to come join us. However, he was plainly skeptical. But curiosity won out since he wanted to see what the strange nice people were up to.

When we reached the place where we no longer needed our horse and drag sled, all of us took off our shoes and stockings to start our journey to the waterfall. We motioned for Sali to follow suit, and so he reluctantly did as we asked. Daddy took one end of the ladder while Sali took up the other end, and everyone rolled up their skirts or overalls and started walking in the stream.

When we came to the waterfall, old Salidonia crossed himself, muttered some sacred words, and prayerfully followed the leader. The men placed the ladder carefully against the waterfall. Daddy climbed up first, followed by Mama, then Lucile, then it was my turn. And, finally, Salidonia climbed up, too. Clearly, he had never seen such crazy people in his entire life, but in no time at all, he was laughing and having as good of a time as we were. We ended up climbing six waterfalls, but the seventh one had us all stumbling, making it impossible to go over or around it.

We rested a while and then we went back to where we had left the drag sled and the horse. Mama and Grandma had put up a scrumptious picnic lunch, and again, we insisted that Salidonia join us. He was flabbergasted, I think, to be included in everything. After that, I think he would do anything for us, no matter how funny it seemed to him at the time. We would camp more at peace than ever before with the purchase of our ranch and having loyal Salidonia looking out for us.

Kendra Blevins Ford

I so wish there was a photograph of Salidonia to share here, as he clearly had a special place in Bernice's heart, but sadly, there is not. He is pictured in my mind as a kind, caring man who had a valued place on their ranch, even if he was "just a foreman."

When we entertained visitors at the ranch, we had the most unusual ways to pass the time. It often involved exploring the property and showing off the waterfalls. Some of the neighbors became our good friends during our time at Valle Vista.

One day, our vegetable man, who supplied us with fresh vegetables, eggs, and homemade butter, asked Mama if we would like to have the dog that always came with him on his visits to Valle Vista. Unfortunately, he informed us that he was going to have to give up his vegetable business due to his wife's illness, as she was not able to be left alone for extended periods of time. The vegetable man said to us, "The dog's name is Mice. She kills 'em, drives off gophers, is a fine watchdog, and loves children. I must find a home for her. Will you take her and give her a good home?" Mama replied, "We'd love to have her!" The vegetable man came over to me, put his hand on the dog's head, patted my head, and said, "You guard her, Mice. She loves you."

They Said She Couldn't So She Did

One day when we were all down at the house, we suddenly noticed sand was sprinkling the window sills, frames, and so forth when we heard Mice barking in a most unusual manner. She was frantic. We had no doubt in our minds that she was calling for help the best she knew how. Salidonia grabbed the shotgun and yelled, "Pronto, pronto!" We heard him, as well as the dog barking, but he ran much faster than the rest of us could and reached the campsite where we slept. There was a large rattlesnake on the ground—right at the head of my bed. Salidonia yelled, "Aqui, aqui!" Mice the dog was jumping every which way across the snake, so fast in fact, that it didn't know where to strike. She made one more jump and then ran to Salidonia and stood by his side. Now, I still don't know how she knew to get out of the way of his range, I suppose we'll never know. She must have seen the gun and instinctively knew help would be coming. Salidonia took one shot and blew the snake's head off.

The previous owner of our dog had informed us that she was likely a cross between an English bulldog and a terrier, an American dog. Some people never accepted this as fact, based on her appearance, but they never saw her in action, either. But this was in 1908, and mixed breed dogs weren't generally accepted as trustworthy dogs back then.

Kendra Blevins Ford

Daddy traveled to Los Angeles once a month to see the doctor and check in with the man in charge of his insurance business. He always had to leave on the early morning train and he would be away for several days. He rode just one train a day, each way. The most unusual things always happened when he was away on business.

One afternoon, we noticed that three men on horseback were coming up the road in a hurry. Not one of us recognized them as neighbors or friends, and neither did Mice. Mama crossed the little bridge with Mice at her heels and the shotgun in her hand. Mice informed them by her growl that in no uncertain terms was she bluffing. One of the men immediately asked, without any introduction, if there were any [Native American] folk around. Mama said, "I'll ask the questions here. Who are *you* and what are you doing on *my* property?" I'm pretty sure that she didn't know how to shoot a gun, but I'll bet you she could have practiced on these squatters. They informed her that they were deputy sheriffs. She retorted, "Well, prove it!" They seemed a little taken aback by this hostile response, but they showed their badges as requested, and that helped us to relax a little. Apparently, they were looking for a man who had jumped off the train by the water tank. He was reportedly being taken as a prisoner to San Quentin. The deputies recommended that we hide all the knives, silverware, valuables, guns, ammunition, and give him anything else he demanded—specifically food or money. We put everything he suggested in pillow cases and put them in a hole that we dug out of the leaves. The leaves were about knee deep on that side of the hill, close to the house.

We were beginning to hope we wouldn't see this wanted man when, just before sunset, we saw a man approaching our camp on horseback. When he got within calling distance the man on horseback shouted, "Mrs. Smith, no need to worry anymore; we captured the man we were looking for." The "wanted man" turned out to be just an almost grown teen-aged boy who stole some stuff from the hardware store, not a man wanted for murder headed for San Quentin.

The next exciting thing I want to tell you about was more frightening than the wanted man scare. At about 10:00 a.m. on one particular day, we smelled smoke in the air. We looked all over the house, the yard, and the barn and couldn't find anything burning. Soon we saw ashes drifting down. When we looked back at the ranch toward the waterfalls, we could see huge walls of smoke in the sky on the other side of the mountains.

Kendra Blevins Ford

Then suddenly we saw some hay wagons with men riding in them coming up to our place. We thought perhaps they were going to go fight the fire. Mama went out to meet them, and they told her that Mr. McGowan, the boss of the Sylmar Olive Factory adjoining our property, had told them that he had seen Daddy get on the train. He knew it was just us women and girls up there alone and might need some help. He instructed us to watch and see how the fire progresses; if the fire came over the crest, we were to load everything we could and take the family down into the valley where it would be safer. We watched very closely— and then the flames came. You never saw so many people move so fast in your life. Grandma was horrified at the way they piled stuff helter-skelter on the wagon and nearly died when two big men just walked over, picked her up and carried her over, and put her on top of the pile of bedding. Mama and I followed, then Lucile and I were helped aboard. We looked around wondering if we would ever see our new house again or the lovely old oak trees, then started to leave. As we turned to take one more last look, the wind changed. Soon, the fire was turned back on itself. Oh, we were the most thankful people. There was no damage at all to our new house and very little to the hillside toward our lovely waterfalls.

They Said She Couldn't So She Did

    A couple of weeks after that, Daddy had to go buy a load of hay from a ranch a few miles away. He said I could go with him, and ride back to the ranch on top of the hay. Boy, that sounded like a lot of fun. He took a huge sheet of canvas and some rope to cover the hay. The farmer had previously informed us of a shortcut we could take, but he didn't say a word about the cactus patch. We soon found ourselves smack dab in the middle of one, a cactus patch that stretched out about four city blocks long on all sides. Only one wagon could pass through at a time. We reached about the middle of it, and I yelled to Daddy, "The load is slipping." He said, "Slide with it, dear. I'll get you out somehow. Keep as still as you can, dear." And slide I did, right into the cactus patch—ouch! Daddy did help me get out of that awful prickly predicament and put me on my tummy to ride the rest of the way back so I wouldn't continue to stick myself with cactus needles. I must have looked like a brand-new kind of porcupine with all those long thorns sticking out of me!

    When we reached home, Daddy instructed Mama to arrange two kitchen chairs facing each other over where we usually tied the horse. Then he had Mama and Grandma sit down facing each other. By the time they had done that, he had picked me up in his arms and carried me over and put me down carefully across their knees, and they began to pick me like a chicken. Somehow, I have never had any desire to go on a hayride after that.

Several weeks later, I told a lie. Daddy decided that called for a good old-fashioned spanking. That's a lost art now. He said, "This is going to hurt me worse than it does you." He gave me what I deserved, then I asked him, "Daddy, can I ask you a question?" He replied, "Sure." I asked, "How old do I have to be to tell a lie and not get spanked? You said it was going to hurt you worse than it does me." Daddy said, "I think I can explain that." He was taken a bit by surprise by this query, but he decided to make his point. He said, "Go get one of those great big needles Grandma uses when she mends things." So I did. Daddy said, "Now stick it right here in my thumb." I reared back and said, "Oh no, Daddy, I can't do that!" Daddy said, "Why?" I exclaimed, "Because I don't want to hurt you!" He just grinned when I finally understood what he meant.

Now, wasn't that a wonderful way to explain why he said what he did? I wish all kids could have as wise and loving parents as I had. Too many parents spare the rod and spoil the child. We have too many overrun spoiled brats who are unloved because they are spoiled. Who loves a spoiled peach? Maybe it was pretty once and sweet. But once spoiled, no one wants it, do they?

Chapter 5

Harvest Time

The house was finally finished and everything was in its proper place, except Lucile's bed and mine. We still wanted to sleep outdoors! Our great big beds were placed on either side of the boardwalk that led into the house. Whenever Daddy ran out of ideas, Salidonia always came up with one for him. Those two men raised up some of the most unusual, one-of-a-kind gadgets when I was a little girl. This time it was Salidonia's contribution: how to make a rain-proof bed. Beyond the point of catching your eye, it was totally lacking in eye appeal, I will admit. It could not be called beautiful, charming, or elegant. It most certainly was distinctive, unique, and indeed, very successful. If you really want one just like we had, simply follow these instructions and make one for yourself.

Kendra Blevins Ford

The picture below is from Bernice's mother's scrapbook and says: Our "Sleepatorium." It is likely a picture of the outdoor sleeping situation she describes below in grand detail.

Get one long-handled umbrella for each bed. Chop off most of the handle, but be sure to leave just enough to fasten to the top of an old-fashioned bed stand. Tie the handle in place with rawhide, and don't worry, if it rains, that will just tighten it up all the more. Now, take two bike-link chains, fasten one end with a swivel hook to the umbrella, close to the part where the ribs are joined. Put the other end to the underside of the bed frame. If done as directed, this will hold the umbrella in place, even in the rain, shine, or wind. The same thing must be done on each side of each bed. Simple, right? Now comes the occupant's instructions. Follow exactly or it will be your fault if you get wet! First, when it starts to rain, lean over the side of the bed and grab your slippers and tuck them in bed under the covers. If you fail to do this, you may step into a slipper full of cold water. Second, open up the umbrella, lean over the side of the bed and try, without falling over, to fasten the hook on the underside of your bed. Got it? Now do the same thing again on the other side. Third, now this is the tricky part, try to get all of the covers where they belong without getting yourself wet. Finally, slide down under the covers with as little motion as you can. It ought to be nice and warm and dry. Now, wasn't Salidonia a genius?

It wasn't long before the days became shorter, the nights longer, and the leaves began to shiver in the trees while eventually scampering down to join their friends on the ground. On one particular Saturday, we went up the canyon to check on the holly forest. Daddy figured it ought to be about ready to harvest, and perhaps the pears, too, over in the old orchard. The south of the canyon was a mass of beautiful and bright, fire engine red berries. Daddy carefully cut several long stems to take to the city to a floral team he knew who bought and sold only the best quality flowers. Then he went over to the orchard on the other side of that hill to see if the pears were worth picking. We hadn't had time to fertilize, cultivate, or irrigate the trees. Goodness only knows when this orchard had any kind of care. We were amazed at the size of the fruit and the quantity. When you'd bite into a pear, the juice just spurted out and ran down your chin. Oh, what flavor! Some were so large, I couldn't hold more than one in my little hands. We picked a few for Daddy to take to a grocer in the city who also dealt only with top-notch quality fruits and vegetables. Some of those pears weighed a pound apiece. This proved to us: dry farming yielded superior flavored fruit. And there were no doubts about the size of the crop. Nowadays we hear so much about "normal" amounts of rain, but no one speaks about "normal" flavor.

Our next dilemma was how to get all those goodies to market. Mr. McGowan suggested we use burros and pack the holly in wreaths, while someone else suggested that we make bales of holly and ship them by trains. We purchased several burros to assist us in the harvest transport. Thankfully, we didn't have any trouble finding a buyer for goods we had to sell. The florist said he would take all of the hollies we would sell him, and the grocer said he would buy the whole crop of pears. Daddy and Salidonia cut the holly with long-handled pruning shears.

They Said She Couldn't So She Did

Lucile and I gathered them up and put them on the dragging sled. When we had a full load, we drove back to the barn. Daddy had made a work table with chairs around it so Grandma and Mama could sit down and make holly wreaths and put them on the burros. We tied and bundled the holly wreaths, placing them alternately: one way had the heads on the one layer, then the opposite way on the next layer. This kept the layers from slipping. For the pears, we wrapped each one in a separate piece of newspaper and placed them carefully: three layers to a box. We ended up packing 12 boxes.

Back in those days, the harvest transactions were never discussed in the presence of children. I have no idea how much money it actually brought to our family. We did repeat the harvest process every year while we lived on the ranch, so it must have been worthwhile.

For three years straight, Lucile and I never slept in the house. As if this wasn't odd enough, I didn't go to a regular school, either; Grandma taught me all the things I needed to learn at the ranch and a teacher in town checked my papers. So, I kept up with the children of my age academically.

During one of Daddy's periodic doctor visits, the doctor said that Daddy ought to drink goat's milk for his health.

Kendra Blevins Ford

Wanting to follow doctor's orders, we knew we needed to start looking for a goat milk source, but we didn't know where we could buy it. We asked around and finally, somebody told us about a man named LaSalle who drove a U-Haul for a living and raised a herd of goats; maybe he might sell us one. So one Monday morning, Daddy, Lucile, and I took off for Mr. LaSalle's ranch. We had to go over the treacherous but historically famous Fremont Pass. (Don't worry; I'll share more about that later on.) We knew Mr. LaSalle was a Frenchman, but we did not know he didn't speak English. It took us much longer to find his ranch then we expected. We arrived at the . . . shall I say . . . wine break. Apparently, this was the respite before lunch. We were invited to join Mr. LaSalle but graciously declined while Daddy explained that it took much longer to reach his place than we had anticipated. We simply wanted to finish our business and get started back home. Daddy told Mr. LaSalle that we wanted a good milk goat, and so one of his herdsmen left to get a goat for us. The herdsman returned with a goat and kid. We didn't want both of them but were coerced to take the kid also. They helped us tie the legs of both the goat and kid so they could not get away (like a hobble), put them in the surrey, and then tied them to the seat.

They Said She Couldn't So She Did

We reached home shortly before sunset tired, dirty, and hungry. Daddy went directly to the house to rest. Lucile told him that she could handle the animals, and so she and I drove the surrey down to the barn. The mother goat could smell hay and was eager to get to it. Lucile got her out of the horse-drawn surrey, put a rope around the mama goat's neck, and then prepared to lead her to the barn. But, Lucile was unaware that you do not lead a goat. The goat led *her* in a straight line to the barn, and nothing was going to stop her! Lucile was, you might say, following the leader—at the opposite end of the rope, sometimes on her back, and sometimes not! All the "whoas" she shouted were to no avail. She didn't know any French cuss words, which might have helped in this situation. Papa and Mama heard the screams from the barn and came as fast as they could. I let go of the kid because I was laughing my head off at the undignified scene of Lucile's handling the animals. We tried to milk the goat, but that didn't go well at all. That mama goat was rather indignant; apparently, the idea of her giving milk to some other little brattish kid was unthinkable! Besides, that "moron" didn't know much about milking. I think the poor mama goat just wanted to go home. The kid goat kept bleating as if it were saying, "me too," all night long. Needless to say, the most horrible, sleepless night was had by all.

Salidonia wasn't home during this time, as he had the weekend off. And, it should be noted, that he had "hit the bottle too hard and someone hit him harder." As a result, he was in jail. Daddy said, "Let him stay there until he can come back of his own power." So, the next day Mama and Lucile decided to take the goats back from whence they came. When Mr. LaSalle saw our rig approach, he was all grins from ear to ear, as he had visions of another buyer. But when he saw the goats, he was a different man. Mother told him the biggest goat was dry, and that we were convinced that the kid was not *her* kid. Because of this, we didn't want them. Mama insisted that Mr. LaSalle take them back and give us a really good milk goat like we wanted the first time. His reply was, "Then I tell the thing . . . I tell the thing that buys the thing that buys it." That nonsense went on and on, over and over, first Mama speaking, then Mr. LaSalle. Finally, Mama said, "Lucile, untie those critters. We will go see the sheriff, and see who buys and who sells what." The old French man certainly remembered all of a sudden that he did have a good milk goat to spare and sent his helper to fetch it. Two men came back, one with a goat, the other with two kids. We didn't want the kids, but Mama was alone and running low on patience, and so she let them tie the goat mother and the two kids to the horse-drawn surrey.

They Said She Couldn't So She Did

Salidonia, Daddy, and I saw them coming up the road. Thank goodness they were almost home! We ran out to greet them. Salidonia took one look and began to scratch his head. Was he seeing things? Daddy was speechless. This time, Lucile let Daddy untie the critters. Thank goodness these three were all one happy family. The mother had lots of milk to spare; she was happy, the kids were happy, and so were we.

Shortly after that, one of the kids ran off, or some coyote had a good meal. Salidonia told Daddy that young kid was as good to eat as a young lamb. The butcher in town assured Daddy that it was true. He also told us that we had the best barbeque cook on our ranch in the whole valley. "You let ol' Sal butcher it and cook it, and you'll have yourselves a little feast. Hmmm! Let me know when, and my family and I will be glad to come over and help you eat it." Well, we did let them know. They came for a goat barbecue, and it was just wonderful. Even Grandma, who didn't know it was one of the goat kids, said, "That meat is delicious! I've got to have a little more of it, please."

Daddy didn't improve as much as we had been led to believe with the addition of goat's milk to his diet. It was decided that we better sell Valle Vista and move into town where medical help was more readily available. I missed the ranch more than anyone. I had not slept in a house with a roof since Salidonia's rain-proof bed was erected. I'm not joking. I think that could've saved my life.

Many years afterward, in fact after World War II, I went out to see the old Valle Vista ranch. We had sold it years ago to Stetson—yes, the Stetson hat family. There was a huge wrought iron gate around the place with a watchman on it. I was told that the current owners were in Europe sight-seeing. I was astounded. How poor the rich people are, and how rich the poor people are. I bet they didn't even know they had a God-made waterfall with maidenhair fern on their property. I'm sure they never walked bare-footed in the stream. And I doubt if they ever climbed a ladder up to a waterfall. I bet they never knew the excitement of getting into a rain-proof bed. Poor souls. Poor people have so many priceless treasures. And they enjoy them.

Chapter 6

Missions

This chapter surprised me as it describes Bernice's profound interest in the historic missions in California. Here, she gives the reader a snapshot of her visits and some interesting lore regarding them. It is uncertain whether she ever worked in them or how often she visited them. Clearly she felt it important to include in her story. As such, I have included this chapter within this work.

In the early 1900s, the whole of the San Fernando Valley from Burbank on the east to Chatsworth on the west was one huge ranch owned by the McClay family. Halfway between Burbank and Chatsworth was the home ranch, at Encino. Then halfway between Burbank and Encino was a large ranch house called East Ranch. Between Encino on the west toward Chatsworth was West Ranch. This divided the whole place into four equal parts. Foothills on the north were the boundary and Ventura Boulevard on the south. At each of these points, crews of 25 or more men and plows would go to the adjoining ranch, have lunch, and return to the original starting point. This was quite a sight to see. It was a long, slow process, because men walked behind the plow, guiding the horse. Following the plowing season, was the harrowing, reaping, and planting. This truly was horsepower plus manpower. There were no women's rights back then. The business of women was cooking for gangs of hungry men. The women did all of the clothes washing; this usually meant hauling the water, stoking the fire to boil the water, and often even scrubbing the clothes. It was a rub-a-dub-dub on a washboard system. The women also put up fruit and vegetables; by this I mean canning and preserving them. Women did all of the baking of bread, pies, and cakes. Women took care of sick people as well as sick animals. In their "spare" time, women made clothes, took care of the kitchen garden, and, oh yes, they kept the coal oil lamps filled, wicks trimmed, and the chimneys shining bright. We had no strikes back then. Everyone was too busy with their own work to bother cutting up their neighbors' successes. "Double talk" was not invented then, nor the fine art of talking with your tongue in your cheek. People did an honest day's work, said what they meant, and meant what they said. When older people say "the good old days," you can see what they mean. We were honest, proud of our homes and families, proud of our country, and worshipped God. What will people say about today's people?

They Said She Couldn't So She Did

The San Fernando Mission was founded in 1797. It was not unusual to seek shelter at the mission. We knew the McClays, and I went to school with their grandchildren and even knew some of the great-grandchildren. Weddings were a cause for a fiesta, and relatives and friends came from miles around to attend one. Charlie McClay was the foreman of the home ranch at Encino. There was a big fiesta I specifically remember and guests were put up at all the ranches. Charlie went to the mission and asked the padre if he could sleep there that night because their house was running over with relatives. The padre said if he didn't mind sharing a bunk with another man, he could put him up in the mission. Charlie told the padre, I'll come in very quietly and won't disturb the other men.

About 4 a.m., a group of men came to the mission and said they would have to check the identification of everyone in the mission (except the brothers of course). Joaquin Marietta, a fugitive, had been seen recently and was reportedly headed this way. Marietta was a famous bandit, a modern Robin Hood. He'd steal from the rich and give to the poor. He was not a notorious killer, but no one ever gave out information about his whereabouts. The group of men believed that this fugitive may have slept at the mission that night. They said, "We believe padre would tell us if he was here, so excuse us please as we proceed with our business." The group of men came to the cell where Charlie was sleeping, recognized him and asked if he had shared the room or bed with anyone. Charlie replied, "Yep. But he left about an hour ago. Do you know who he was?" The men replied, "Well, Charlie, we think you might have just shared your bunk with Joaquin Marietta."

I have visited many of the missions throughout my life. The one at San Miguel was also founded in 1797. I made a watercolor painting of it a long time ago. The Missions San Gabriel, Monterey, San Rafael, Ventura, and San Diego are all kept up in amazingly good repair. The Santa Barbara mission has never missed a religious service to my knowledge since it was founded. There used to be metal poles with mission bells on each one, along the Camelia Rio. Reportedly, the wealth that the mission padres found was used to build and establish the missions. Since the invasion of the hippies, these have been destroyed.

The historic unrest of Valle Vista ranch was in Fremont Pass. It has an interesting history, as well as being known as extremely dangerous. A man by the name of Pio Pico was causing some trouble with the United States Army back in 1831. General John C. Fremont was sent out in 1841 to take over the job of letting General Pico know he was not welcome on California soil. General Pico was on the San Fernando side of the mountains. These were the same mountains back at our ranch. Word was sent to General Fremont that General Pico was setting up an ambush at a place where one could cross the mountains. General Fremont took his men to another place, and with picks and shovels, they cut out Fremont Pass. The Americans were not able to get behind Pico. However, Pico saw the Americans and the pass that had been created and had no other choice but to surrender to General Fremont in 1846. The grade was so steep over the mountain that horse-drawn freighters often could not hold their wagons and their own animals were often run over. Many men were also run over by their own wagons because the rocks were not able to work as a chuck during descent from the top of the mountain.

Chapter 7

Rae Lake

The picture above says: Upper Rae Lake- the most lonesome and fearful beautiful spot. Bernice describes a family vacation in detail within this chapter. Her mother had kept a scrapbook long ago and many of the photos within it are from the trip to Rae Lake. The scrapbook page pictured here is just one of many that have been preserved from over a hundred years ago.

After we had lived in San Fernando for a while, we made many new friends. One of them told Daddy about a wonderful time he had had when he and some friends had gone on a camping fishing trip for several weeks, up to a Rae Lake, which sat off the back of Mount Whitney. Daddy was feeling fine and plans were blooming for all of us, except for Grandma, to go up to a lake for an entire month. We invited a close friend of Mama's to join us. Grandma had a sister she seldom saw, who lived in Phoenix. Arrangements were made and so Aunt Emma came over to stay with Grandma while we were away. Our fine neighbors said they would keep an eye on the two older ladies and see that they had no problems while we were away.

Aunt Emma arrived about two days before we were to leave. We were all excited about our upcoming trip, but Lucile, in particular, was carried away with the idea of going somewhere by "pack train." Huh. I didn't see what was so wonderful about that. Goodness gracious, didn't everyone who went traveling *pack* their things on a *train*? I knew enough not to say anything or I'd be laughed at or teased.

Daddy and I took the horse and buggy down to the packing house to get some fruit to take on the trip. We took one flour sack and filled it half full of lemons, tied the middle, and then filled the rest of it up with limes. The next sack we filled halfway with grapefruit, tied it and finished filling it up with oranges. You won't believe this, but it cost us fifty cents a sack!

At last, the big day arrived, and we took a train to Mojave. We had to change to a narrow gauge train at Owenyo. Unfortunately, that train connection was not at the station yet. We were told that everyone had to get off at Owenyo. The conductor told Daddy, "Put your belongings on the freight platform, mister; there ain't no hotel here. Them bunk cars over there are the only hotel, and them is for men only." Two or three of the men said they were going to go see the sights of the town. After they left, Daddy said, "I'll show you the real sights of Owenyo."

There was nothing else to do but roll out our bedding and sleep on the freight platform with the sky over our heads for a roof. Soon Daddy came over and said, "Look where I'm pointing; that's the Big Dipper. Here is the Little Dipper. There is the Bear. Oh, look! That's a shower of stars. Now watch the little stars; I do believe they are twinkling with laughter at us for sleeping in Owenyo's outdoor sleeping room." Those stars looked so close, you could almost believe you could touch one if you tried. The "real sights" of Owenyo, California, I shall never forget.

They Said She Couldn't So She Did

Our narrow gauge train arrived at about 7:30 in the morning. We were glad to get settled on board before it became hotter. Even leaving that early, it was already pretty hot. About four seats ahead of us was a redheaded man snuggled down in one great big seat. The engine of the train was belching soot and smoke. We had to make a choice: open a window and never look like a light-colored person again, or leave the window closed and melt. This was a very strange kind of a train; only one car for people but there were lots of box cars, flat cars, and a caboose.

The higher the altitude that we went, the hotter it was. We ran out of drinking water, so Mama asked Daddy to get some grapefruit from our food supply so we could share them and quench our thirst. I was sure that Daddy, who always fixed things, could do *something* about that awful heat. So I asked him to do something about it and to please hurry. Daddy replied, "Do you think it might help if I threw that redhead off the train?" In half a split second, the redhead began to grow bigger and bigger, in fact about six feet bigger. I had never seen a giant before. Suddenly, I forgot all about the heat. Now, I was worried about that "redheaded giant" while chills were growing up and down my spine. Daddy whispered to me, "Do you think he will throw me off the train?" I wasn't sure but I wasn't taking my eyes off of him for a second. He got up and stretched, and I let out a screeching yell for Mama. The giant looked at me and smiled. If he had touched me, I'm sure I would have fainted, no joke about that. He told Daddy who he was, and said he knew this part of the country very well. We didn't know it then, but this friendly giant was to become my brother-in-law. His name was William Beam, and a finer, kinder man you won't find anywhere. He had two sons, Warren W. Beam, a big man, and William E. Beam, both just wonderful people. Bill, as we soon called him, gave us the name of a very fine packer and guide, a Mr. Parker. Bill suggested we see him before we saw anyone else about taking over the management of our trip. He was telling us that if he "doesn't give you the best time of your life, I'll come up and find out why."

As soon as we arrived at Independence, Daddy went about to see this Mr. Parker who had been recommended to us. He said that if he was to be the packer and guide, then we would leave everything to him. He would furnish us with a guide as needed, animals on the trip, and even do the cooking. In fact, he would purchase and pack all of the food we would need, as he could do all of this faster since he knew the best deals and where things were sold that we would need. He said, "Remember, I'm an experienced man in this kind of work, and I will have to be the boss." So, we turned over everything to him and let him do his best work.

We were to leave early Tuesday morning. We were told that all that we would have to do is to have a hearty breakfast and leave the place clean for someone else to use. At last, the great day arrived. We were excited as we could be. All of sudden I heard the tinkling of a bell and then I saw them. I ran as fast as I could to tell the rest of the family, "Look, it's a bunch of men with large mules and huge horses and they even have bells on the mules!" Daddy said this was right, *this* was the pack train. I thought Lucile had gone off her rocker. *That's* the PACK TRAIN? Oh, that's a pack train!

Kendra Blevins Ford

(The picture below is of the pack train that Bernice is referring to, found in Bernice's mother's scrapbook.)

I never saw so many mules in all my life—or such big horses, for that matter—and there was even one very small donkey for me to ride. Everyone thought I'd love that little donkey, but he looked so insignificant to me. Well, one of the pack train guys named Mike came over to me and told me very confidentially, "You are very lucky. Molly is the smartest animal of all!" Everything was put on the mules, and one of the guides, named George, started us off. The first mule had a bell on its neck, then behind all the mules came Daddy with Damaris sitting on the most beautiful gold-colored horse. And my goodness, it was huge! Aunt Carol, a friend of Mama's, came next in the order. Then Mama, Mr. Parker then Lucile, then the tiny donkey and me. Mike was always the last one in the pack train.

Mr. Parker had told Daddy on the previous day that a group of young men had traveled to the opposite end of the lake from where we would be staying. They will be going hunting and should be within calling distance if we should need them. He also told Daddy that the lake had been stocked with trout and then completely forgotten and unfished for seven years. What good fishing we had in store!

We rode about 20 miles that first day of the trip. That would prove to be the longest, yet easiest ride of the whole trip. Mike, Molly (the donkey), and I were always the last ones to get into camp. Or any time they stopped to rest, for that matter. This bothered me greatly because I had always been taught not to be late and not make anyone wait for me. I wondered what Mama was going to do about this. I told Mike in confidence my concern, and he replied, "Well, Mr. Parker is the boss, and he told me to take care of you, and that's what I am going to do."

Mr. Parker cooked supper that first night; what a relief that must have been for Mama not to have to prepare a meal for so many people when she must have been as tired as we were.

Kendra Blevins Ford

George unloaded the mules, unsaddled the horses and fed them, and then hobbled them. This was something new for me to see. In case you don't know what hobbles are, they are like handcuffs on prisoners, but they are put on the feet of the animals so that they cannot go very fast or far away. We ate and then turned into our beds, as we knew we had to make an early start again. The second day would not be as long mileage-wise, but it would be profoundly slower, for the sake of all the animals. We would be climbing not mere hills, but mountains: the High Sierra off the back of Mount Whitney. We had to ford many streams, swift and roaring, though not very wide. It looked so terribly dangerous to me. When I saw that great big horse Daddy and Damaris were riding sink to the belly in the water, I was scared stiff. I thought my little donkey and I would sink out of sight! My fear must have communicated itself to Molly. She was just not going to go near that river. I was panic-stricken. All of my folks had gone off without me. Mr. Parker came back to see what the problem was. He picked me up, put me on the horse with him, and we rode double every time we had to cross a stream. He told Daddy that I was shaking so much; I almost shook him off the horse! They had to tow Molly across the larger streams.

They Said She Couldn't So She Did

(The picture that follows is also from Bernice's mother's scrapbook with the inscription: At the Summit of Oak Creek Pass, at the highest traveled peak in North America.)

We had to go over Oak Creek Pass, which at that time was the highest traveled pass in North America, elevation 12,800 feet. Going up, we had to zig-zag back and forth, as we were above timberline and it was all shade. Small slabs of smooth stones almost as large as a small pancake were a perilous terrain, the poor animals would go up three steps and slide back two.

By the time Mike, Molly, and I arrived, George had hot tea and hard tack ready for us to snack on. Mama was not that fond of letting her children drink tea! However, Mr. Parker explained that with all of this stress, strain, and the highest altitude she can stand, this hot tea will do much to not only warm all of us but soothe our nerves, so you must let her have some. Daddy agreed by saying, "You are absolutely right, Mr. Parker, and we will accept your guidance in all matters." After we had our good hot tea, Mr. Cochran gave each of us a large padded square of canvas and a big horse blanket safety pin. "Put these on like diapers. Watch the horses. You will do as they do. No one can ride the animals down this part of the mountain, it is too steep. The mules, the horses, and even Molly sit on their rump and slide down like kids. I expect this to be the longest, fastest slide any of you have ever experienced. It is 600 feet to the bottom!"

George had hot soup and hard tack for us at the bottom of the mountain. While we were enjoying our soup, we heard some beautiful bells ringing; both of the guides as well as Mr. Parker rushed over to get their binoculars and began searching the mountains that we had just slid down. You could say we were in the bottom of a bowl. The mountains looked like they were straight up and down; in fact, these mountains looked like spears trying to pop balloons made of clouds. Those bells were mysterious to our whole family. Finally, Mike said, "I see it now, it's another pack train." He fired the shot and we heard it echo from all sides. It was amazing. Mr. Parker had wondered if the bell-like toll was from the other pack train party that had gone by the day before. They might have had to return for some unforeseen reason, we were told. We would never leave an area after hearing a bell from another pack train until we were satisfied beyond a doubt as to the cause.

It bothered me to see all of my folks get so far ahead of us. Mike was kind enough to understand my unease. He asked, "How would you like to learn to read trail signs? They aren't like city street signs, but we have good signs here on the trail. See that little pile of rocks on your right, now quick, look across the trail. See that one? That means to look for a new sign on your left. When we get to where there are trees, you will see a mark on a tree called a blaze, and remember, always listen for the bell on the lead animal. It if comes nearer, then stop, and wait for whoever that is to pass you, if the trail is wide enough. They will do the same for you because no one comes in here without a guide."

We soon were down where there were trees again. Mike told me he knew where some of the best gum you've ever chewed grew. You could pick from my gum tree if you want to. I thought to myself, gee whiz! I had never picked any gum before. Well, I soon learned that this "gum" was actually hard sap from spruce trees, but I liked it.

Mr. Parker had caught a fine mess of trout for supper. We were not too tired and sat around the campfire and lingered for a little while. Suddenly we heard a scream, like a woman's. It came two or three times. I think we all were a little surprised that neither Mr. Parker nor Mike went to her rescue. In two minutes, we heard a shot fired. Then George fired a shot in the air. They explained that it was not a person who screamed, but a bobcat! One of the men at the other camp across the lake had fired the first shot, so we responded with a gunshot, as that is how they did things in this outdoor setting.

The next morning we were up early again so we could reach our permanent campsite by midafternoon. The pack train men set up our camp: they looked over the land for us, cooked a fine supper, and made our beds on pine boughs. My, but they did smell nice! Mr. Parker and George left with all the animals except Molly, who stayed with us, in case we needed to return before our scheduled time, and Mike stayed in case we needed him.

There were tiny streams close to camp, which washed away some of the soil, so the banks overhung the sides. I actually flipped a fish out with my bare hand, on the opposite bank, but it flipped back in before I could grab it. It truly was a real fisherman's paradise. Daddy made a fishing pole for me out of a small branch of a tree. He put some string on it, and a large bent pin for a hook. "Those fish will grab anything that's put in front of them," he said.

Gradually, with Mike's gentle understanding ways, Molly and I became friends with him. He showed me where there was something growing that I could rub on my hands, arms, and neck to keep the mosquitos away. He let me pick some and I enjoyed the "new perfume" that grows right outdoors. "Now do go and sit next to your mother," he said. "When no mosquitos start to bother her, tell her you know how to keep them away, and you will get her some if she really wants it." This plant was called pennyroyal.

The young men at the other end of the lake came over to invite Daddy to join them on a hike to hunt deer. He said that he didn't think he ought to go on a hike, and thanked them for the offer. "But I tell you what," he said, "on your return, stop here and have supper. We'll keep it hot; no need to go to your camp to wash up. The water is just as fresh and just as cold here and you might be tired.

Kendra Blevins Ford

The hunters returned late in the afternoon with two deer. Mama had prepared fish and hot cornbread like only she could make, with vegetables and coffee to accompany it. The next day the hunters brought us a fine hunk of venison. Oh, it was delicious, cooked over an open fire.

We stayed for a whole month at the lake. Before we knew it, we heard bells ringing again and a hearty, "Hello, hello? Anyone home?" There was Mr. Parker, with his mules and horses to take us back. Our 30 days had flown by so fast! I do believe, however, that everyone was a wee bit anxious to sleep in their own bed, eat at a table, and enjoy an honest-to-goodness soak in a bathtub, even my sister and me. Rocks and stones had no heart for anyone's bones.

This trip had so much pure joy in it. The memory of those things will linger on for as long as I live. I cannot see the stars twinkle or hear the trees hum sweet tunes with a little breeze since I live in a city now.

I trusted Molly more now [on the way back], and *almost* trusted Mike as much as I did my own daddy. This time during the ride, I didn't have such an avalanche of strange sounds or things descending upon me, one after another, faster than I could keep up. Mike didn't tease or scold me. Rather, he helped

They Said She Couldn't So She Did

me understand strange things like fear. I hope that now he is my age, someone has been as kind and helpful as he was to me. This little verse came to mind; I don't know who the author is.

A fishing pole is a curious thing,

A piece of wood and a piece of string.

On one end a child with a great big wish;

On the other end, a tiny little fish.

Chapter 8

What Do I Do Now?

Bernice is pictured above, circa 1913.

They Said She Couldn't So She Did

Lucile graduated from high school and went on to junior college. I was in high school then, but I didn't like it, as none of it made sense to me. I'd been having *terrible* dreams every night. I dreamed that Mama and Daddy would go out the door and were *never seen again*. I was so upset, that I dreaded to go to bed at night for fear I'd wake up and find it was not a dream, but true. How could *I* take care of my baby sister and Grandma? Lucile never seemed to be in these dreams. Finally, I just couldn't stand it any longer. I went to Daddy and told him all about it. I told him I wanted to drop all those "useless things" like ancient history, Latin, Greek mythology, and algebra. And instead, I wanted to take typing, shorthand, and other business machine operations, which in my opinion were *useful* classes. He told me to finish the term out and then we would talk about it. At the end of the term, we moved to Eagle Rock, California, so Lucile could go to Occidental College. I continued to have those awful dreams.

One day, I asked Daddy for permission to go downtown on the streetcar and look for a job. I missed Valle Vista and my friends so much because they had never teased me. I was lonely and bored and needed something to occupy my time.

Kendra Blevins Ford

I believe it was around this time that Bernice's parents allowed her to quit school entirely. According to census documents I reviewed on www.ancestry.com, Bernice only completed three years of high school and never "graduated." She was, however, a firm believer in learning new things and doing work that was meaningful, and that seemed to help her throughout her life regardless of what situation she found herself in.

Daddy let me go but told me not to worry if I didn't get a job the first time. *Sometimes people have to look for a long time to find one*, he told me. I went downtown, but I didn't get a job on that trip.

The next morning I went down early to one of the big department stores. There was a girl standing by the door. I asked her if she worked there. "No, but today I will see Mr. Smithers and I will be hired." I followed her like a shadow.

She walked into the department store and stepped up confidently to the lady at the counter. She informed the lady, "I have to see Mr. Smithers today." She was immediately told to go right through the swinging gate, to be seated, and in two moments Mr. Smithers would come out. We both went in. Soon Mr. Smithers came out, looked at the other girl and told her to come into his office. That left me sitting alone and wondering what I should do now. In two moments I found out. Mr.

They Said She Couldn't So She Did

Smithers came back out, looked at me and said, "Come on in." He looked at his desk and said kindly, "I do not seem to have your name here." I replied, "No sir, I've never been here before. I want a job here, though, very badly." To this, he replied, "I'm sorry, but I never hire anyone without experience." I tried again, "May I ask you a question please, sir? If I had lied and said I had the experience, would you have hired me? How can I get experience if you do not hire me? How can I ever honestly say, yes, I have the experience, if you won't give me a job? I don't care what kind of work it is, I'll work hard, and learn quickly, and you do not have to pay me very much. Won't you please give me a chance?"

He hemmed and hawed. "Well, uh, come with me, I'll see if I can find something that you can do." He took me to an enormous room filled with adding machines. He spoke to a pleasant-looking woman who came over to me and led me to a long table full of baskets that were filled with little bundles of white paper fastened with rubber bands. I learned that these were the sales slips from each department of every floor. Mr. Smithers provided the following directions: *Take one bundle at a time, add up each slip, and write the total on the bundle. Do the same thing to the next bundle. When every bundle has a total on it, go to the adding machine and add all of the totals. Then take the rubber band off, and add up each slip again. That gives you the whole total. That is double-checking your work, which is required. Next, you are to separate these little bundles by the sales clerk's number, and then add each one of these on the comptometer. That total should be the same as the long tape on the big adding machine.*

Mr. Smithers stressed to me, "Go slow. Do not try to keep up with the other girls. You do not need to do a full basket in one day. Go slow, and do it correctly the first time. If it is not correct, you will have to do it over until you get the same total twice. Remember, you are just new. Go *very* slowly. And in time, you will just naturally do it faster. I know you can do it. If you are not sure, just come find me. Good luck!"

I couldn't believe it. I had a job! It would pay me $7 per week! I was so glad to go home and tell Daddy that I had landed a job. I was proud that I would not only be earning but also learning, while Lucile would only be learning in college. Mr. Smithers told me up-front that he would not be able to keep me on permanently, and that he would have to let me go after Christmas. It was currently July.

Daddy said that he was proud I had not given up the first time that I was turned down. He asked if I would do something for him—to promise that I will never give up learning as long as

They Said She Couldn't So She Did

I can still hear, see, talk, walk, or write. I'll never forget his words: "You may be too young to learn, but you will never be too old to learn." I have kept that promise to this day and have learned something new every year. I started to go to night school and learn typing, shorthand, and switchboard operation in hopes that someday I could be a fine statistician.

Remember how I've said that I always was a sickly child and went to sleep with Daddy holding my hand? About this time, Daddy became very sick and it was my turn to sit by him and hold his hand. Only he didn't wake up. That was September 30, 1915. There was only one way to break the generation gap: by silent communication, acquired by holding my hand.

In January I was laid off; kind Mr. Smithers sent for me and said, "You may be asked for references at your next job. If so, be sure to give my name. I would be most happy to help you again. Now you go out of here with your head held high. You can now honestly say that you have had office experience, so good luck to you and goodbye. Oh, here is your paycheck and a good luck piece." The good luck piece was a brand-new $10 bill.

The next position I filled was with a physician, who made me ask for my paycheck every week. I found this quite degrading to have to beg for money that I earned. Mr. Phillips, a fine friend of my parents, helped me in business matters, and so I told him how I felt about this issue of asking for my pay. He said he would come over and talk with me about this situation. In our meeting, he wrote a letter to the doctor on his legal letterhead, informing the doctor that his secretary was a daughter of Graham Smith, an officer in the Masonic Lodge. Mr. Phillips suggested that he treat me with respect, and not expect me to beg like a dog for my paycheck; he also suggested that the physician change his ways immediately. Mr. Phillips was an attorney and was unafraid of speaking his mind. Mr. Phillips said that I should go to work as usual but work just as well as ever.

I was instructed to adhere to the following: *When it is time to leave, if he makes you ask for your check, do so and take it, but then say that you will not be here to work with him on Monday, since you have a position with better pay in a lawyer's office.* Well, it turned out that I had to beg for my paycheck again. Then I told him just what Mr. Phillips told me to say. The doctor looked at me as if I had jabbed him in the stomach and his jaw seemed to have hit the floor.

Mr. Phillips told me when I first began working for him that I should keep my eyes and ears open in case I might thereby learn of some kind of work that I might like better. *If you want to*

They Said She Couldn't So She Did

find out about a different kind of work, he said, *just tell the girls here that you are going to see about a job. Your dad would have done the same for my daughter if I'd had one. You might have to work a long time before you find just exactly what kind of work is best for you.* It turned out that I worked for him for about three months.

One morning, while I was on my way to work at Mr. Phillips' office, I saw a very interesting headline in the newspaper that someone was reading on the streetcar. I wanted to see the whole article, so I hopped off the streetcar at the very next corner, bought a newspaper, and read the headline: *United States Navy Enlisting Women in Washington D.C.* I was astounded, inspired, and speechless. Women in the Navy!

Upon entering my workplace, I informed the girls in the office that I was going to see about enlisting in the Navy. My boss came into the office shortly after this announcement, and so I told him about what I had read in the paper and stated, "You know that we don't have any men in my family to serve our country, so I just have to go!" I immediately went to the Navy recruiting office.

When I arrived at the recruiting office, I discovered that there was a long line of men that went from the elevator in the building up to the recruiting office. Impatient, I just barged right in ahead of the men, which wasn't very nice now that I think about it, but I had something very important on my mind, and I couldn't waste any time. There was a small, gray-haired gentleman behind the counter. When I approached the counter, he came over and asked if there was anything he could do for me.

I'd never seen so much gold braid on a uniform. It reached from his elbow to almost the wrist. I thought he must have been an admiral. (Of course now I know he was a chief petty officer, a yeoman, and each gold hash mark was for four years' service.) He had gold bars on his uniform, too. I asked if he was in charge, and he said: "No, ma'am, but maybe I can help you." My reply was, "I want to join the Navy." To this, the officer replied, "Sorry ma'am, we do not take women in the Navy." Undaunted, I replied, "Well, I beg your pardon, sir, but they are enlisting women in the Navy in Washington D.C." I showed him the newspaper to prove it. I stated again, "Now, if they can do it, so can you."

Suddenly, everybody stopped what they were doing and came over to read the newspaper I held, even that civilian who had been sitting in the corner. This civilian suddenly came to life and grabbed the chief by the arm as well as *my paper*, and said,

They Said She Couldn't So She Did

"Wait til the old man sees this!" I thought that was pretty nervy, so I followed right behind them, but they didn't know I was there.

When they reached the room they were headed for, this civilian said, "Captain, you've got to see this. There is a dame in the office that wants to join the Navy. She told the chief they were doing it in Washington D.C., and he told her he couldn't do it and she came right back at him, 'Well, if they are doing it in Washington, there is no reason why you can't do it here.' Here is the paper she had; take a look at it." The captain replied, "Well, what's her name and where is she?" So I stepped right out in front of them, and stated, "My name is Bernice Smith."

The captain hemmed and hawed and said that I couldn't do it, that I would not be allowed to enlist in the Navy. To this, I retorted, "Well, if they're doing it in Washington, you can do it here." Then he explained he had to have authorization and would have to send a wire. The civilian again took charge you might say, and said, "Captain, if you get a gobs hat, a blouse, and a pair of pants, and tell her to put them on in the doctor's office, I'll make a poster that will turn this town upside down!"

Now, I think the captain was trying to buy some time. He asked if I wouldn't mind putting the clothes on. Well, I didn't see anything wrong about it, so I did. The civilian was Howard Chandler Christy. I didn't think much about him at the time. He had just grabbed my newspaper without asking for it, and I certainly didn't like that at all. I wasn't in any frame of mind to hear a lot of excuses, either. While I was getting into the duds, I made up my mind what I was and was not going to do. Once I was dressed, I returned to the Captain. There was a huge canvas cart piled full of mail, right next to the captain's desk. I walked over to mail, looked at it, and said, "If you ever get that authorization by wire, and get me a table and a typewriter, I can start answering some of those letters. I won't charge you anything. Say, I might as well get to work right now. You see, we have no men in my family, and this is the first time my country has been at war, and you *do* have someone who wants to help." The captain retorted, "I cannot enlist you without permission. You might say that I'm not the boss and I have to take orders. Now, I can do this: if you don't mind my calling *you* a typewriter, I can charge the amount I would have to pay to rent a typewriter, give it to you, and give you lunch chips until we get authorization." I replied, "Well that's fine with me. I must go back over to the office where I work and tell them I won't be back. Don't worry, I'll come right back here. So, get a table and a machine so I can get to work."

They Said She Couldn't So She Did

Incidentally, the "old man," the civilian that I referred to, was not an old man at all. Quite the opposite, to be truthful. He was a well-renowned illustrator who was commissioned to create recruitment posters for the Navy; I just happened to enter the recruiting office at the same time he was there.

(The navy poster on the following page is a personally signed copy addressed to me, her first great-granddaughter.)

GEE !!
I WISH I WERE
A MAN
I'd JOIN
The NAVY
BE A MAN AND DO IT
UNITED STATES NAVY
RECRUITING STATION

They Said She Couldn't So She Did

When I returned to my workplace and told him what had occurred, my boss asked, "How much is the Navy going to pay you?" I replied, "Well, they didn't say, but how much do you pay for the rental of a typewriter?" My boss chuckled at this statement. "What? I *buy* my typewriter. Now, Bernice, you go back and help them, but you come back here before you go home. You understand?" I decided he sounded a little bit like my dad so I found the time to come back as Mr. Phillips had asked me to. Someone in the office must have telephoned the recruiting station and found out what the pay would be. They informed me that the base pay was $96 a month, plus $60 for a voucher and subsistence, making it total $156 per month! Now, that was quite a difference from the $60 I was currently earning. There was also another $25 per month due to me since my mama and my little sister were now dependents of mine, upping the total amount to $181 per month. To think that I started my first job making just $20 per month! Wow, that pay increase is not bad. I felt like I was about to become a millionaire.

Bernice's first "dog tag" (shown on the next page) which was hand written rather than typed, with her fingerprint appearing on the reverse side. The May 7, 1917 date must be the day the tag was made, which is prior to her "official" enlistment date noted in her story. The "97" is for 1897.

My civilian boss was delighted with the progress I made with the Navy. I officially enlisted on May 14, 1917, as Yeoman (F), first class, United States Naval Reserve Force. After I'd been in the naval reserves about three months, I took an examination, passed, and I was named Chief Yeoman, female. I also believe that I was the first woman in California to enlist in the Navy. Other cities began enlisting women a short time after I enlisted. We were called yeomanettes and did office work, and there was no time to waste. After about six months at the recruiting station, I was transferred to the Naval Reserve Training Station in San Pedro. However, I actually worked at the submarine base because the Naval Reserve Training Station was being deactivated at that time. This made for lots of opportunities for people to work. At first, I was the only female among 2,000 men on base; I was glad to see some other women arrive shortly thereafter.

Kendra Blevins Ford

Bernice D. Smith's Official Navy Yeomanette Portrait

They Said She Couldn't So She Did

There were some old-timers on base; one was a chief with 32 years of service under his belt. He was sure the Navy was going to the dogs with skirts on duty! But, there wasn't a thing he could do about it. However, he thought he had a solution. He was the one in charge of setting up the watches. The crew was divided into two groups: the port watch and the starboard watch. I overheard the chief say, "I wonder what them skirts will think when they have to stand watch just like we do?" One of the men chuckled and said, "I'll learn 'em something." So they went ahead with their scheme. They made up a watch since it was Thanksgiving week. The made-up "watch list" was posted down on the bulkhead wall of our office. Everyone was buzzing around it. Someone said, "Hey, Shorty (as I was called in the Navy), did you know your name is on the watch list for Thanksgiving Day?" Not knowing any better, I replied, "Well, what do I have to do?" The man replied, "It just means you have to come to work the same as usual, only you'll be the only one in the office. And you won't have your mess hall. I expect someone will bring you something to eat for lunch." To this, I said, "Okay," and promptly went back to work speaking to someone on the telephone.

So, I went to work on Thanksgiving Day just like any other Thursday. I was busy typing out a monthly report when the door opened and in came Captain Shepherd. I was the only one in the office, so I stood at attention. The captain stated, "At ease. What are *you* doing here, and what is your name?" I replied meekly, "I'm on duty, sir." The chief barked at me, "Who said you were?" And so I replied by saying, "My name is posted on the watch list, sir." The captain was thoughtful for a moment and then said, "You cannot have your dinner in your regular mess hall, you know. I'll have to have it sent in here to you. When you finish eating, report to the O.D. Give him your name, and you'll be relieved from duty. The O.D. will have my car brought around for you and you will be taken home. I do not approve of this at all. I will not have women standing watch on my base." Rather surprised, I simply nodded my head and eked out a "Yes, sir! Thank you, sir." Well, I had a most delicious Thanksgiving dinner with *all* the trimmings plus a ride home with a chauffeur, in uniform, no less! The captain sent for Chief Chappell the very next day. When he came back to his desk, which was near my desk, he came over and apologized to me. At that base, I was the only woman to have ever stood watch on a holiday.

One Saturday morning, we were all standing there waiting for the captain's inspection to start. It was hot, and the uniform for the day was whites. My office opened out to our breakdowns and some of the officers came in out of the sun and perched on top of the desks! I was busy typing and paid no attention to the officer sitting atop my desk. That is until I heard a voice . . . "What the hell!" Apparently, someone had upset an ink bottle and the captain didn't notice it until the cool ink penetrated his white starched uniform and little pants inside. I said to him, "Captain Maxwell, if you can go into an officer's cabin and snag all the garments with ink on them, and bring them out to me as fast as you can, I bet I can get that ink out and get them back to you in time for inspection. He hurried and sent the clothing back to me. I went into the galley and found it empty. So, I let out a "someone come quick and help me" and just like magic, three heads popped up out of the deck. I told them: I need a pan of buttermilk. They said they didn't have any. So then I asked them to please give me a pan of milk and a bottle of vinegar. Now, I told them, do not put all of the clothes into the pan with the milk and vinegar. Just rub the sour milk thoroughly on the ink, then wash just that part with soap and water. Now get all the soap out and iron those places dry. Please do it on the double and then bring them out to me. Indeed they did; in fact, they did perfect work. One of the officers took the garments into Captain Maxwell; they were steaming hot from the ironing. The servicemen came out laughing their heads off. He would henceforth be known as "Hot Pants Maxwell."

Kendra Blevins Ford

About this time, I went back to living at home with Mama. Lucile was teaching in Arizona. I had to commute back and forth to San Pedro. There was a very nice-looking, pleasant chief warrant officer who had to commute to San Pedro also. We often talked while waiting for the streetcar at a transfer point. I didn't know his name at the time, as we had not been properly introduced. One day he came over while I was standing there waiting for the streetcar. I was watching a cute little white kitten playing with its tail and being funny. Suddenly a dog appeared and someone sicced it on the kitten. Quick as a wink this officer made a grab for the dog, caught it, and got the kitten out of its mouth, but it was too late. The little neck was broken. He went over to the gob who had sicced the dog on the kitten and told him, "I'm putting you on report for cruelty to animals." The officer was Harrison Halsted Blevins, my future husband. I thought then and still think to this day, he was one of the finest men I have ever met. *(Harry's Navy portrait appears on the next page.)*

They Said She Couldn't So She Did

Chapter 9

Navy Wife

Harry and I went together off and on for about two years. We decided to tie the knot and were married on July 9, 1921. Lucile and her husband Bill Beam share the wedding date with Harry and me, as we had a double wedding.

Bernice did save the wedding announcement for this double wedding, but sadly there are no photos of the two sisters on their wedding day, nor of the early days of their marriages. She did not provide any wedding details in her recordings that would have been interesting to hear, unfortunately. The details of her honeymoon, on the other hand, are noted in the paragraphs that follow.

Harry and I went camping on our honeymoon. There were many places that neither of us had ever been, so we made the most of it. I expect most everyone has heard of dismal plans. Well, we certainly had our share. We were looking forward to digging our own clams and having clam chowder. I was not about to tell my new husband I didn't know how to make clam chowder!

We found a good place to set up camp. I suggested he set it up and I'd go get the groceries. Harry said that he would and that he would talk to a fisherman about the proper time to dig clams.

I hurried over to the grocery store in high hopes of seeing someone who looked like a good cook. Now, how do you tell a good cook by looking at her? You don't. You have to have that most valuable, God-given gift, women's intuition. Thank goodness I had it or maybe just plain good luck played a role. While I was dashing around, gathering the necessary ingredients, I saw a white-haired lady and I asked her if she knew how to make good clam chowder. She did, and so she told me how.

I caught a fleeting glimpse of my new husband in the grocery store, and, ducking out of sight quickly, I made myself scarce and started back to the car. Soon he caught up with me. The fisherman had told him that we could not find any clams until the tide changed. Harry had bought a can of clams, so we had chowder anyway.

We decided to go for a swim. The sand was so nice and clean, but as soon as you stepped into the water, it was very uncomfortable on your feet, just full of sharp rocks and stuff. Harry stepped on something sharp and bent down to pick it up. Lo and behold, it was a nice big clam! He dashed up to the car and came back with a bucket. In no time, we had a bucket full of clams. But I decided that I just had to have *one* more. I bent down to grab one, facing the shore. When wham! That seventh wave knocked me off my feet and I fell to my knees letting go of the bucket of clams. Harry grabbed me and wrestled the bucket, but all the clams fell out. In no time, we had it full of clams again. The seventh wave is supposed to be the biggest wave, then there will be six smaller ones. But beware of that seventh wave!

We left the next day to go to Governor's Camp near Santa Cruz, California. The redwood trees there are reportedly the tallest in the world. The Mariposa Grove in Sequoia National Park has the largest in circumference. The campsites in 1920 were not equipped with hot water; it was tepid, not exactly cold, but it didn't encourage you to linger longer. There were heavy cement laundry tubs and washboards, and a few laundry lines to hang your laundry on. There was a charming little stream running through the camp. The most delightful lodge was built right over part of that stream. The tables were set on either side with lovely maidenhair fern on the backs of them.

They Said She Couldn't So She Did

The food was exceptionally fine. At one end of the lobby was a huge fireplace where everybody could be warm if it was cold or rainy outside. We would have enjoyed staying longer, but once we had seen all we had decided to see, we had to move on the next morning.

Next, we went on to San Francisco. Large cities do not appeal to me. They are too noisy, smelly, and windy. We did have a couple of redeeming features here, though: a bathtub with plenty of hot water and a nice place to eat.

We had a marvelous seafood dinner the last night we were in San Francisco. This was in July, and so everyone and their brother was out to go someplace it seemed.

We left early the next morning to have the car overhauled: greased with a complete lube job, brakes tested, etc., as we were planning to go up into the mountains and we were not too sure about the availability of any mechanical help up that way, should we need it. As our luck would have it, road repairs, as usual, had to be done every so often and we had to wait in line for our turn to go under these controls. In those days we didn't have paved roads as we do now.

Kendra Blevins Ford

Similar to "road construction" as we know it today, during this time period they called it "road repairs" and people were forced to wait for the repairs to be done before they could continue down the road.

Nearly everyone got out of their cars to stretch and chat with the car nearest them while we waited for the repairs to be done. The car in front of us was, you might say, different. It had a chauffeur in uniform and bejeweled females, not mere people. The car behind our Ford was loaded down with a jolly bunch of young fellows. They were having a high old time of it. A couple of them rode on the fenders. The center of the road was higher than the sides. The wheels were in ruts. And sometimes the pan of the car would get hung up on the center part. When this happened, everyone in the car behind it would get out and help push the unfortunate car over the hump. You guessed it. The society dames' "special car" got hung up. The chauffeur was fit to be tied. Those dames were unreasonable. The young men behind us scampered up to us with gelled hair, saying, "Come on, guys, many hands make light work. Let's get the uniformed gentleman out of the mess before some of the females chew his head off." Someone suggested, "It might help if the lovely ladies would get out." But they disdained to do so. I'll never forget what happened. As if they had been drilled to do it, every guy,

They Said She Couldn't So She Did

including my new husband, Harry, lined up like pallbearers and lifted the car, screaming dames and all, up and over the hump.

When we reached Truckee, California, I decided to make stew and dumplings for supper. We had just finished eating our stew when some people came to the camping area next to ours. They looked so tired. Harry went over and asked them to come on over and have supper with us because it was still hot, offering to help them set up camp after they'd eaten. They were glad to come over. The next evening, they had us over for frog legs. I'd never eaten them before, but they were delicious.

We went fishing and caught lots of trout. The water was so clear, we could see the fish swimming up to the bay, and now and then turn away in disdain. This would be our last evening at Lake Tahoe.

Our next place to visit on our camping honeymoon was Yosemite. We left early in the morning, so we could find a nice camping spot. One of the highlights of our trip was the fire fall. Up on top of Glacier Point, there was a vast amount of pine cones gathered. In the evening, just before dusk, all visitors were urged to gather and hear a lecture by one of the park rangers. While everyone was listening to him, other rangers set the pine cones afire and just shoved them over the granite cliffs. Our attention was turned in that direction by the most beautiful voice, no doubt it was a recording of Nelson Eddy's rendition of "Indian Love Call." That was the famous fire fall. It was quite spectacular!

Time was passing by so rapidly, we had to leave shortly after that fire fall night in order to get back to L.A. and start looking for a place to rent, either in San Pedro or Long Beach. We found a comfortable place in San Pedro and lived there a couple of years. I had to learn to drive as it was necessary for me to take Harry to the naval base when I needed the car to go grocery shopping.

One day I drove Harry down to the naval base, and when it was the usual time for him to come home in the evening, I drove back again to pick him up. I waited and waited for him. I noticed that no more boats were bringing in officers. So I thought about this; then I went and asked about him and found out that he was not on board. He had gone out in the morning on one of the submarines but had not returned yet. I left word for him to phone me, and that I would come and get him when he did get in.

I waited a couple more hours and then phoned again. I was told, "We have been trying to raise the ship since 2 p.m., and they are out between Catalina and here." Well, I waited for two more hours and got the same reply. Then I did go into a tailspin myself. Not too long before this, a submarine had been rammed and sunk. I was currently pregnant but had not told Harry yet. And now that this was happening, I was scared to death. We had some fine local friends, so I phoned one couple and they came over and stayed with me. I later learned that in this case, "raise the ship" meant contact it by radio, not to recover a sunken submarine. Apparently, the whole electrical system had gone out for some unknown or unexplained reason. The submarine that Harry was on was without power of any kind. Boats were sent out to find her and tow her in. Well, what an initiation that was!

One time, Harry's ship had gone to sea and had been away for three months. Nearly all of the Navy wives and families followed the ships as they travel. Harry had sent word through my mama (and my sister Damaris) to join Graham and me to come out to Harry's ship off Santa Monica pier and have dinner together.

At this time, Bernice had her first and only living child, Graham, but did not mention his presence in her recordings until now. I feel this is the most logical place to put in a few photos of the early days of their marriage, when Graham was a baby. The first photo is from the day she brought

Kendra Blevins Ford

Graham home from the hospital. The second is a snapshot of Harry, Bernice, and Graham together as a young family.

They Said She Couldn't So She Did

Since Harry had "the duty," he couldn't come home with us during this time. When the rest of our family and I were ready to go home, Harry asked a fellow officer to help show him to dockside.

There was a speedboat session on the water. On the way in from Harry's ship, Graham (who was only two and a half at the time) fell asleep from the gentle rocking of the boat. As we approached the pier, I woke Graham up. A speedboat sped in front of us, and every boat was bobbing to beat the band. A show officer helped my mother on to the floating dock; she took two steps and tried to hang on to something, but there wasn't a post or anything handy for a land lover to hold on to.

Kendra Blevins Ford

Damaris had scrambled up as a youngster would. The officer placed the baby on the bobbing dock, and he started to toddle to his grandma, lost his balance being half asleep, and fell into the water! I yelled to him, "Swim to Mama, Graham, swim to Mama!" The boatman and the coxman jumped overboard, but apparently, they couldn't swim. They held on to the piling and tried to catch Graham. Meanwhile, my unattended launch was moving farther away from the pier. Finally, a policeman dove into the water from the top side of the pier. He missed landing on my baby by inches and grabbed Graham while he was going under for the third time. Then I yelled for help, and in no time at all, someone managed to grab one end of the boat with a boat hook, or whatever you call it. Graham wasn't hurt, but was he mad as a hatter! Apparently, he had lost the little flag that his daddy had given him. Just a year previously, we had lost our second son at birth. This scary event brought that memory back like a tidal wave.

In the summer when Damaris was out of college, she, Harry, Graham, and I drove up to Gold Beach, Oregon, to visit with Mama, Lucile, Bill, Juan, and Billy. We had a fine trip up the coast. After we had been up there a day and a half, Harry said that he had gotten an official wire and had to go back to base. We drove him over to the station in Roseburg, so he could go back by train, and Damaris and I stayed in Oregon a few more days. When we decided to leave, we took Mama up to Crater Lake with us, and from there to Planet Falls, then finally to Grants Pass, where she could get a bus home.

Most of the Navy wives follow the fleet wherever it goes. The fleet was preparing to go to Honolulu, Samoa, New Zealand, and Tahiti. Most of the wives would go to Honolulu and stay there until the fleet returned to Hawaii and then returned by Navy transport to California. I had been counting the days until this trip, and it had all been arranged. Then, two days before everyone was ready to leave, Harry informed me that he had to draw most of the money out of our bank account. The story was that his mother had made a pledge to a church and she needed the money for that, and Harry gave it to her without question. Needless to say, I no longer had the money to take the trip to Honolulu with the rest of the Navy wives and families.

Can you even imagine the hurt and disappointment that you would feel if this had happened to you? Bernice does not give any other details surrounding the money incident. Her printed words as shown here barely convey the raw emotion I heard in her recordings.

I didn't say a word to anyone. But the day the fleet left, I left also, but in the opposite direction. I drove to Portland,

Kendra Blevins Ford

Oregon, to visit with my sister, Lucile, and her family. We took many trips down to the beach to pick the wild blackberries, canned the blackberries, had picnics, and ate wild strawberries. Lucile's family was going to pile into my Model T Ford with Graham and me and go on a Mount Hood loop trip. But unfortunately, one of Lucile's boys became ill, so Graham and I went alone. We went to Vancouver, and then over to Victoria.

When the ship was out on this long cruise, Harry and a young chief whom he had trained as a radio operator, worked out something very fine. Harry and the young Chief Boyd had been experimenting with attaching the telephone with the radio (I believe) to see if one could actually talk back and forth. He worked and experimented with the equipment and tested it on short distances. Then when his ship left for stateside (we called it that, back then) they decided to test it out every night and see how far away they could be heard clearly. When the ship was entering the Golden Gate, Harry was down in the radio shack and saying to Boyd at Pearl Harbor, "We are just entering the Golden Gate." At that precise moment, the executive officer stepped into the shack, and he promptly demanded a satisfactory account of *what is going on here*! It surely was not according to Navy regulations for Harry to phone me from the ship at this distance. Harry had the executive officers talk to Boyd. Then the executive officer told the commanding officer about it. He came down and talked to Boyd. The commanding officer made an official report of this unusual thing. Harrison Halsted Blevins received a presidential citation for this new communication discovery. But that isn't all.

A short time after this, Harry was again down in the radio shack, and an S.O.S came in. Harry immediately took charge. He received permission to instruct the radioman on the ship sending out the S.O.S to hook up the radio and telephone in accordance with his instructions. Also, the radio operator on the two ships nearest the distress signal was instructed to hook up to the San Diego Naval Hospital with the chief surgeon on the line. This resulted in a conference call of three top naval medical officers in a diagnosis consultation of a sick crewman on a small naval vessel without a medical officer on board.

A hospital crewman on the small craft had the earphones on, and step by step operated on the ill crewman while in direct communication with the medical officers. From the nearest vessel came alongside the medical officer who made an examination of the patient and his report was that the operation was a complete success. Only God knows how many more lives have been saved by this radio/telephone gadget.

When I lived in Sequim, Washington, I was telling this story in one of my social groups. One of the ladies said to me, "That sick crewman was my nephew." None of us are perfect, but some are more wonderful than others. Harrison Halsted Blevins, Commander, USN Retired is one of the most wonderful men the Navy has *ever* had. Do not let any of your children or their children forget it.

They Said She Couldn't So She Did

Harry came home one afternoon around four o'clock and told me that he was being transferred to Brooklyn Navy Yard in New York. The Navy packers would be here tomorrow morning at 8 o'clock. Harry declared, "You will have to have everything separated into three separate piles, things that belong on the ship with me and later for housekeeping, things we won't need for a long time that can come later by transport, and things to go with you and Graham until the ship arrives. You will leave Los Angeles (we lived in Long Beach at the time) at 5:30 p.m. First, you will go to Omaha, Nebraska, and stay with my dad. He is very ill and I cannot get leave. You are to stay with him as long as he lives. Eleanor, his sister, will stay with you. Then, you will go to your folks in Kentucky."

For the first time ever, I traveled alone, on a train overnight, with a toddler. From a very early age, Graham had been taught to not be destructive with his toys. Because of this, he was terribly frustrated when the train "broke" into two pieces and the engine went "away." He walked back toward the rear end of the train with me and I was expecting to see other coaches added. But no such thing. "There goes my bed!" he wailed, when that part of the train was separated, poor little tyke.

My turn for real frustration came when, unbeknownst to me, the regular engine was switched to an electric engine. (I had never been on a subway!) I avoided tunnels as much as I could and never talked to strangers. I did what I was told to do and didn't ask questions. When we left Cincinnati, I was told to go to the St. George Hotel. In the morning, when I looked out of the train car window, I saw we were in a tunnel. I got up and dressed as fast as I could, then got Graham dressed also. That tunnel was endless!

I asked an old lady how to get to the St. George Hotel since there were no railroad men to ask. She told me to go get some tokens and take the next train with the green lights. I did, even though there was not a motorman or conductor in sight. I had no way to know on which street to get off! Worse still, we were not out of that tunnel. That train went full blast. It just flew past platforms where people were standing. At last, I asked the lady standing next to me if she knew where to get off. "Right here, hurry! Hurry!"

We managed to get off that busy subway. I saw a wall of people get off of an elevator, so I rushed over to it. No elevator operator. The doors suddenly opened. Someone had pushed the right button. We were in a huge place. I went over to the counter and asked the lady, "How do I get to the St. George Hotel, please?" She replied, "This IS the St. George Hotel!" That was music to my ears.

About that time, I kept thinking that it was all a horrible crazy dream. It just could not be! I had gotten off one train, taken another train, and landed in the hotel lobby, in the one hotel I wanted? How could that even be possible? I also learned that I had gone under the Hudson River! We stayed at that hotel for about two weeks and then found a nice apartment to settle into.

Our new apartment [in New York] was only about nine or ten blocks from a pretty little city park. One night it snowed, and it was the first snow fall that I had ever seen. I woke up Harry but he wasn't at all interested in that wonderful sight. The next morning, after Harry went to work, I took Graham to a small store around the corner and bought a sled. I put him on it and pulled him about eight blocks to the little park. I never in my life had so much fun! We both got on the sled and went down the hill in a flash, then I pulled him back up. We just went up and down over and over. Time just flew! I did get home in time to do the dishes and clean up the apartment before Harry came home so I could tell him how much fun we had.

I talked Harry into taking Graham and me over to Central Park in New York City with the new sled. Poor Harry. I don't believe he ever had much fun as a boy growing up like climbing waterfalls or playing in the snow. It was like pulling eyeteeth to get him to get on the sled and ride down the hill as the other daddies did with their kids. I suppose he thought it was undignified and not to be done by a naval officer, even if in civilian clothes. But I told him I was going to go down if he didn't. He didn't want to see his wife go either, so he went. From then on, he *really* had the time of his life. Now, who do you suppose wanted to go to Central Park the next weekend?

At last, we were sent back to California. Graham and I traveled by train, as most of the other officers and their families went back that way, too. You often hear people speak of a ship as "*she*." I was convinced Harry was married to "her." Harry did have a girl in every port. "*She*" was the ship he lived on, worked on, understood, and loved. Nothing, I mean *nothing*, could compare. I believe now that we ought *never* to have married. We definitely could have been congenial lifelong friends, however.

I always wondered what happened to Bernice and her first husband, Harry. All of my life I knew her under the name of "Great-Grandma Tongate" and wondered why they were no longer together and didn't carry the last name of Blevins, my maiden name. Clearly, she had deep respect and admiration for Harry. It is unfortunate that their marriage could not handle the numerous separations that they undoubtedly faced during his time in the Navy.

We lived in Long Beach for a while. Then we went to San Diego. On Wednesdays and Saturdays, if Harry didn't have duty, I would pack a picnic lunch and other foodstuffs for a beach supper like fresh eggs to bake in seaweed leaves, potatoes to bake on hot driftwood coals, and a campfire coffee pot *(oh,*

They Said She Couldn't So She Did

that smells so good!). We would put our bathing suits on at home (Graham and I) and stow the fishing gear and poles in the car. Then we drove down to the wharf to get Harry. From there, we drove over to La Jolla coves. We caught fish and then cooked them for supper—from the ocean into the frying pan. Those baked potatoes and eggs with sliced tomatoes, lettuce, and cucumbers sure tasted good. This, I think, was the only time Harry *really* enjoyed being with the family. Maybe the salt air made him feel more at home. Harry was always at ease and jolly when on board ship.

    The time came where we needed to decide whether our marriage had the strength to continue. We talked it over and decided there was no use in trying to go on with our marriage. His ship would soon leave for Panama. And when it sailed, it would be less of an ordeal for all of us if we were separated. I decided to file for divorce. Harry said he would not contest it. Harry paid alimony. When he came back from Panama, he used to come to my house to visit with Graham. He has married again.

Chapter 10

Leucadia

This chapter is quite interesting to me as my great-grandmother and I share a love of flowers. I know she would adore this picture of purple coneflowers, grown in my garden.

I was fortunate to have some very fine friends in San Diego. May and I served together at the submarine base, and her husband Jack was our paymaster. She and I were out of the service now and her husband was retired. Navy people have a nice way of helping former shipmates out if they can.

May and her husband knew of a young woman named Amy who was looking for someone to take care of her mother who had a place large enough for both of them to stay. They thought taking on a boarder might help provide an income while also allowing Graham and me to stay in our home. I also would have a sitter in place if I needed to go somewhere. It seemed to me this idea of roomer and boarder could be the perfect solution to both additional income and an occasional sitter.

I found a house that filled the bill perfectly. Upstairs there was a nice bedroom with a bath next to it, and across the hall, there was a larger bedroom with an adjoining room. This, I thought, would be nice for the daughter to have. One room for her living room, and the other her bedroom. The mother could have the bedroom nearest the bath. Graham and I would have the whole downstairs to ourselves.

Everyone seemed to be delighted with the arrangement. May and Jack said they would do my grocery shopping for me if I didn't have a car. However, it turned out that the mother was bedridden, needed food every two hours, and could not get in and out of bed without help. This I was not told. She could only eat the most expensive cuts of beef. Pot roast, stew, or homemade vegetable soups "did not agree with her." She had a little bell to ring if she needed me. One morning, she had given me a very bad time of it, ringing that bell constantly. I had taken her lunch up to her, but she said she didn't like it and wanted something else. Three things happened simultaneously: Mrs. Adams rang the bell and I went up to get what she wanted, the ice man came in through the back door while May and Jack came in the front door, and I fainted and fell down the stairs, scattering the dishes along the way! The ice man, as well as May and Jack, found me unconscious on the floor. Mrs. Adams was ringing that bell furiously. Jack ran up and told her to stop ringing that bell. She flew into a rage and ordered him out of the room. Saying, now she knew why I hadn't answered the bell. Jack told her, "Don't you ring that bell another time! Bernice is unconscious; she fell down the stairs. My wife and I heard the crash! Now you keep quiet until your daughter arrives." We phoned Amy and told her, "Get an ambulance over here immediately to take her mother to a rest home, hospital, or even a hotel, but get her out of here, now!" Jack and May stayed all night with me.

May had her hands full. May's mother and Jack's mother were living with them. Each one wanted the other one to get out, however. This had been going on for a long time. Jack and his mother left; he gave May a divorce and custody of their son and the property.

They Said She Couldn't So She Did

So then Jack and his mother came over to see me. She was in her 80s. He had rented a small house between San Diego and Oceanside. His mother was not able to do the housework and cooking any longer. There was a small house close to the one they had rented; in fact, the two backyards joined. Jack wanted to know if I would like to rent this little house at a lower rent than I was currently paying, and let them take their meals with me. It would help both of us. I decided to do it.

Jack built himself a lath house, made some flats to plant flower seeds, as he grew everything by seed. I have never been a person to sit and do nothing, and I like to learn new things. I would go over and help Jack weed the flowers, transplant the seedlings, and ultimately learned all that I know now about raising flowers for a wholesale or retail market. I quickly learned that it was a very interesting occupation and one that was also profitable.

About that time, the government gave all World War I veterans a bonus. I spent part of mine renting a log cabin flower shop on the main highway. Jack and I decided to split costs 50/50 as well as the profit. He took me up to the best-known florists in the Los Angeles area. I learned how to make floral arrangements for funerals, corsages for special occasions, as well as table arrangements, both formal and informal. I learned the floral business from the ground up. I operated the retail shop, kept house, did the washing and ironing, as well as the cooking, for Jack and his mother.

None of this constant, hard work was acceptable in the eyes of my family, however. All they could see was that Jack was the former husband of a good friend of mine. He and May helped me when I needed it, and I would have been a heel if I didn't help him and his mother. Maybe if I had never been a divorced woman, they would have been able to see things through my eyes.

They Said She Couldn't So She Did

A treasured memory of happier times: Bernice's Mother, Emma (left) and Bernice's sister, Lucile (right).

Despite the ill feelings of my family regarding my divorce, I sent a roundtrip fare to Mama for a visit; she was living with Lucile in Oregon at the time. I had her come down for a visit with me on Mother's Day. That was a waste of time and money. I never saw her again. I was a disgrace to the family because I was a divorced woman, therefore could do no good.

Many readers may find these words appalling, (as did I), but unfortunately, during this era, women who had been divorced were disdained,

Kendra Blevins Ford

even shunned, by some of their families. What a vastly different world we live in today.

  I called my shop *The Little House of Flowers;* the little shop was situated on the highway and had a plate glass window across the front of the building. There was also a barn out back behind the shop. The inside of the shop was painted seafoam green, or a very delicate shade of apple green you might say. There were small, low tables, with dull black edges scattered around inside the shop. Close to the big window, there was a beautiful shadow box, all in pure black; the outline was shaped like a picture frame with mitered corners and overhead, there was a concealed light.

  Floral arrangements in those days were more of a draped effect, not a precise shape. We used tall baskets, large pottery, and glass or china vases. One morning, on the opening day of the shop, I put a large silver basket with red dahlias, gladiolas, and ferns in the black shadow box setting. A local businesswoman drove by and told the people in the bank where she worked that I had a marvelous display of red flowers in a silver basket. One of the customers came by (I knew both women) and said, "I heard you had a beautiful display of red flowers in a silver basket in your window. I wonder if Marie is color blind?" I chuckled in reply, "Oh no, I just sold that basket

They Said She Couldn't So She Did

with the red arrangement and have substituted a bronze basket with orange and yellow flowers just now."

That shadow box was the talk of the area. Some thought I had a design painted on something like a window shade and just pulled it up and down. The third day the shop was open, there was a funeral for a lovely young girl who was killed by a drunk driver. Everyone in town went to her funeral. I had to hire a truck to take all of the floral displays that I had made up for funeral orders. People told me afterward that my pieces were outstanding. I also furnished flowers through Weckstrom's in Del Mar, in the shopping place called Twin Oaks. Jack and I leased a strip of land between the highway and the railroad tracks, a full seven acres, and grew all of our flowers there, except ferns. We had a supply of flowers the whole year round. We shipped flowers to Los Angeles and San Diego. The flower business was doing fantastic, but unfortunately, my son was not.

Being on the coast, we had a lot of fog in the air. This high moisture climate was not helping my son thrive. Graham took a bad cold and nothing we did helped him. He coughed incessantly day and night. The doctor said I had to take him to a dryer climate or it might turn into tuberculosis. He recommended Prescott, Arizona. I had never been there before.

Kendra Blevins Ford

Jack knew of a very prominent woman there named Grace Sparks. He contacted her and asked her to be on the lookout for a house for me. Sadly, I sold the flower business, rented a small trailer, and loaded it up with our beds, bedding, dishes, and a couple of chairs, just enough for the short term until my furniture could come over by Bekins Moving Company.

I have been a lifelong aficionado of all things green and growing, especially flowers, so here is yet another interesting parallel in the lives of Bernice and me. While listening to her account of giving up the flower shop, I was rather saddened to learn that something she loved so much had to be given up for the sake of her son's health. I do understand where she was coming from as I also have sons (and would do whatever necessary to help them, at any cost), but I haven't been faced with needing to move out of state to improve their health, either. This is another interesting part of this era: physicians were highly revered and whatever the doctor told you to do, you did without question and without a second opinion. My, how far we have come in that regard!

Jack drove us to Arizona as I still didn't have a car. His mother visited friends until we could find a place for them to live since I was moving away. Grace thought in a day or so there would be a place up near her house ready for me to move in to. It was being painted, inside and out. When we were halfway to

They Said She Couldn't So She Did

Phoenix, Graham went to sleep and finally stopped coughing! He just couldn't be wakened even to eat, poor child! He was completely exhausted.

Grace talked the owner into letting me place my things on the sleeping porch and put a rush on the painting so I could sleep in the house and use the kitchen by Monday. It all worked out just fine. Grace had room at her place for Jack to stay overnight. Graham and I stayed in a hotel until we could access the house on Monday. On Monday, Jack returned to Los Angeles.

Chapter 11

Prescott

Prescott, Arizona, was up in the mountains, over the white spotted grove. It was a mile high, lovely pine trees all around, wonderful air, and the nicest people you'd ever want to meet. Thank goodness it was not a big glamorous city! It was clear that the people of Prescott respected the beauty of God's making. They didn't cut down trees, then put saplings in tubs to have tree lines made by a middle man.

Our home was to be on Pleasant Street. It was up a long hill. I'll never forget that first heavy snow. The street was officially closed off so no motor traffic could cross it at the bottom. At the bottom of the hill were flat trucks that the kids climbed on and they and their sleds were towed up to the top of the hill. Up there at the top of the hill, a woman kept a big bonfire going. You could roast your own hot dogs or marshmallows or you could even have free hot chocolate and

They Said She Couldn't So She Did

donuts! There was no solicitation of any kind. Grownups just pitched in and made it a wintertime picnic. Some people even lent sleds to those who didn't have any. You don't often see that "let's all give the kids a good time" atmosphere, and for free, mind you. That was in the Depression, and yet you never saw so many happy people having a good time together.

Jack and his mother came over and spent Christmas with us, to see how we were doing without any friends or family nearby. On Christmas Eve we had a real blizzard. I had never seen such a sight! It snowed so hard you could hardly see across the street! The wind was blowing fiercely, its tone deafening.

Early in the morning Jack's mother, Mrs. Dunnegan, got up out of bed, lost her balance, fell, and broke her wrist and her pelvis. I called the doctor, and he came over right away to see her. He said he thought it was unwise to try to take her to a hospital. "She's better off to just keep quiet and comfortable as possible. You will need to keep her bed linens and clothing dry." He arranged a daily laundry service to help me out with this task. Needless to say, I didn't get out very much. Poor Mrs. Dunnegan was humiliated about having to have her bed linens changed so often, but she was physically unable to control her bodily functions.

Kendra Blevins Ford

One day Grace Sparks came and brought her mother over with her to chat with Mrs. Dunnegan while Grace and I went for a drive. We drove out into the country and passed a charming ranch. On our way back, we stopped to look at it; I was delighted to see that it was for sale! There were five acres, with the whole five acres bordered by poplar trees. There was a hurricane chain fence all around the whole property.

The chicken house was an enormous 25 feet by 125 feet! Each 25-foot space was partitioned off; this made three sections with roosts and nests for chickens, one for incubators, and one for sacks of feed. One section had two small doors so the chickens could be let out to eat fresh food outdoors—first one side, and then the other. The outside yard was growing in between the trees. There were peach, apricot, and plum trees on both sides of the whole chicken house. There was a marvelous berry patch loaded with raspberry, boysenberry, blackberry, and strawberry bushes. I could have all the fruit I wanted and put up [preserve] a lot of it. And if I could grow my own vegetables, what a help that would be on the food bill! Maybe I could even market some of the vegetables for sale or trade them for staples I need. The lawn in front of the house was egg-shaped, with whitewashed rocks, and pretty little window boxes for flowers by the windows.

They Said She Couldn't So She Did

The next day I went to see the banker about the property. I learned that they had foreclosed on the former owner. This was during the Depression, and properties were selling quickly. I talked the banker into selling it to me for no down payment and $50 per month.

Dr. Southworth said that Mrs. Dunnegan could not withstand the trip back to California. I asked him if she could stand the short drive out to the ranch in Chino. He said if we packed her in like a piece of china, she'd probably do alright. Well, we packed her in between towels and bedding and drove very carefully with no sudden starts or stops. Jack carried her to the car and then carried her from the car to the house. By May, she was able to walk a little. Her wrists had mended, and she was able to knit again. We were quite surprised yet pleased to see her make such progress.

Unfortunately, Jack took to drinking heavily, to the point of being an alcoholic, so I told him that he would have to leave my ranch. And so Jack drove his mother back to Los Angeles, and I never heard from either of them after that.

My ranch was located about 15 miles from town. Because I didn't have a car to drive back and forth now that Jack and his vehicle were no longer there, I had to give up the lovely ranch and move into town. Graham and I looked around at what was available and found a cute little place in town that we thought would suit us well.

One morning in December, I woke up with a very bad sore throat. My good and faithful Dr. Southworth had been killed by a drunk driver, and so I asked around and someone gave me the name of another doctor to try. I called him. He came to the house to check me over, gave me a shot, and said I better have someone take care of me for the next few days since I was pretty sick. He sent a retired military nurse over to take care of me. I was getting worse by the day, however, and she said I ought to have another doctor check me, too. She called one she knew. He came in, took one look at me, and said, "Why isn't this house quarantined? Are there any children? If so, where are they? Who is your doctor?" He was furious. He called the doctor I had and told him to come over immediately. He read him off but good and he had the perfect right to do so! I had *scarlet fever*! Graham was in school when all of this happened. He was kept in quarantine at the house and was not able to go back to school. There I was, with Christmas just around the corner and not able to go to town and buy anything for my son. Not only was he banned from school, but also no one could come in or even near the house. The grocer left the groceries at the foot of the hill and

They Said She Couldn't So She Did

Graham would go get them for me. The grocer supplied my groceries on credit since I couldn't write a check for him during this time.

I phoned my sister Lucile in Los Angeles and told her what was going on. Graham had nothing to do at the house and was rather bored with no friends to play with. I asked her to send something over to help keep him busy that would be fun. She sent him two model airplanes, which turned out to be the perfect gift. He just could hardly put them down long enough to eat or even go to sleep! He had a fine time with them. For Christmas, she sent him six to eight different kits. Everything in a good-sized box. Each plane was in a separate Christmas wrapping, so it looked like a lot of Christmas presents around the tree. There were some small packages, too. The instructions were to put these in the bag, and draw out one each and see what you get! I got a bottle of airplane glue, Graham got a string of pretty beads. Some packages were a few nuts or bars of candy or gum. She went to a lot of trouble to give us something to laugh about.

Eventually, Graham had about 24 planes and then he built himself a hangar out of a cardboard box and a fine landing field. He had a grand opening for this. The doctor and nurse were the only people who attended the grand opening, but they were good sports and made him feel like he was something very special. Indeed he was; he was very exact about his work also.

When I recovered, the doctor said I could not continue to live at that altitude. I also had Graham checked out; he even had a chest x-ray, and there was nothing to worry about there. And so, as soon as I was up to packing and so forth, we went back to L.A.

Chapter 12

Los Angeles

Graham and I realized that the noise of the city was quite difficult to get accustomed to after experiencing the peace and quiet of a small town like Prescott, Arizona. Familiarity tends to bring you back to what you know, so that is why we returned to Los Angeles, despite the inherent busyness, smog, and noise of a big city.

My sister Damaris was engaged to a man named Peter Craig. She and I thought it might be nice if she stayed with Graham and me until they were married. By sharing a third of our food bill, she would not have to pay out so much for food and rent, and she would have more money for her future wardrobe. There was no one to stand and hold expenses for her wedding, unfortunately. Mama had died, no money was set aside for a future wedding, and my income was meager. I did, however, manage to give them their wedding breakfast. There would only be the bride, the groom, and his parents, plus Graham and me. They were married in Santa Ana, in the little church they attended. They knew of a fine place with excellent food, where the wedding breakfast was held. They went to Big Bear on their honeymoon. Both Damaris and Peter were working; he was a Ph.D., actually, and taught fencing; two of his most famous clients included Douglas Fairbanks and Errol Flynn. Peter had been fencing for years and was actually ill as a result of it. He was ordered by his physician to eventually give it up, but I never did know why.

Graham and I did not enjoy living in an apartment, smelling what everyone else was having for supper as well as the usual apartment noise. We went house hunting yet again and found a nice little place. The former owner must have bought two lots, side by side. Right down the center was a very wide driveway with two separate garages, with a house in front of each of them. There was a nice-sized living room/dining room combination, kitchen, one bedroom, and a huge sleeping porch on the back. The tenants in the other house used to keep an eye on Graham because I worked swing shift at the post office in Los Angeles. I had breakfast with him every morning. He had a paper route, so he was up early for that. He knew that if he got sick all of a sudden, he was to go to Lavonne next door and she

They Said She Couldn't So She Did

would contact our doctor's number as well as my number at work.

Graham still enjoyed making model airplanes. Other kids would often ask him, "How do you do that?" So, one day I had a grand idea—that Graham might like to have a model airplane shop of his own. In addition to supplies, he could teach the neighborhood kids how to make the airplanes. The kids could come and go into the shop by an outside entrance, eliminating the need to go through our house.

Graham put up a sign between the curb and the sidewalk with the name of his model airplane shop: Model On. I helped him get stocked up with supplies to start with: paper, paints, kits, glue, and everything else they could possibly need. We had work benches with plenty of space to work on and places to store unfinished planes in. (*Graham is pictured on the next page with his largest plane, ever.*)

Kendra Blevins Ford

The model airplane shop was very popular in our neighborhood. All of the mothers knew exactly where their sons were when they weren't at home; they were at Graham's shop. One father didn't know about the shop, and he scared me half to pieces one day when I caught him peeping through the French windows trying to see where his son was. I stepped to the front door and asked him what he was looking for. After the peeping incident, all of the kids pestered *that dad* until he finally bought a model plane kit of his own and began to work on it. Then he challenged all of the other dads in the neighborhood to make a plane that could beat his!

The boys had competitive airplane contests frequently, and it is no surprise that we didn't have juvenile delinquency problems in our neighborhood.

They Said She Couldn't So She Did

One day, I decided to surprise Graham and make a model airplane myself and fly it. *(Bernice is pictured above with her airplane design.)*

There was no racial or gender discrimination in our neighborhood during this time period; we had people from all different cultures and races: Japanese, [African-American], white, man or woman, and we all lived in harmony. One of Graham's steady customers, an [African-American] boy, came over for something for his model plane, but Graham wasn't home at the time. I was available, so I sold him the supplies that he needed. When that was completed, the boy came over to see what I was making. I made him promise not to tell Graham or anyone else: that I was making a model airplane. "I'm going to make it and fly it in the next contest," I told him. He gave me a big grin and said, "You ain't no way gonna show nobody how you gonna fly that plane 'cause you've got the wings on backward!" He had a good laugh about that. Before we could get those wings off and put on right, Graham came home.

I've never been one to just sit idle; I just couldn't stand sitting around. I told some friends about my desire for something to do and they gave me some interesting ideas to consider. One of my friends suggested that I buy some land, build a duplex to help pay for things. I could live in one side and rent out the other. A property that had enough space so that I could have my own garden and grow my own fruits and vegetables . . . I could just taste the strawberries I would grow. Oh, I could hardly wait!

This is yet another trait that I share with my great-grandmother. It is rare for anyone to find me sitting around with nothing to do! I have many hobbies that give me joy.

I found a commercial acre out on Foothills Boulevard, not too far from Valle Vista, my old childhood home. I could see the lovely mountains in the distance and that was a great comfort to me. Graham and I decided to put up a lath house with a suitable counter so we could sell flowers all day. Not having a good ladder that is long and strong, we decided to put up one whole side of the building at a time. I think that must have been a former version of a pre-fab building; we dug the post holes for the one side of the building and were measuring to put the other two post holes in just the right place. We had a long measuring cable, the kind you wind up. Graham had dug one hole, and put the measuring tape down and told me to hold it tight so he could measure it perfectly. A breeze came up and I just couldn't hold that measuring tape. We were both exasperated, and with somewhat of a slight temper, Graham came back with a hatchet in his hand and said, "Now, Mama, hold it tight right here," and he brought the hatchet down with a mighty bang, sharp edge down, right there, where he wanted it. Neither of us could believe our eyes. We just about laughed until our sides split. He had cut the measuring tape in two.

We put up that one side, then on to the next piece. I was supposed to hold up one end across my shoulder, while he guided the other end into the hole. He kept yelling, "Hold it higher, Mom." I kept getting weak in the knees, took one more step, and went down. Unknown to us, there was a bum hitchhiking along the road who had been enjoying himself, laughing so hard he could hardly stand up. We stuck with it, and after a while, we both learned, if you keep at a thing long enough, all you will lose is your patience.

Just a short distance from us, there was a Japanese family with a nice garden. They were very quiet people and minded their own business. One night there was some very unusually heavy traffic on Foothills Boulevard. We were awakened by yelling. When I looked out the window, I could just make out men with guns who ran up two steps and fell down, then they would get back up and do it all over again and again. They were yelling at the top of their lungs; it seemed to be directed toward the Japanese family's house. At first, I wondered if it could be paratroopers, as this was right after Pearl Harbor. By morning light, we could see they were American soldiers, kept posted all around us. The old river aqueducts were just a few miles from us; no doubt the soldiers were there to protect it, as well as the highway, the railroad tracks, and the tunnels because the trains would be vital for troop movement.

After this scary episode, Graham and I decided that it was not so good for us to be that far out of town. I saw an ad in a paper that someone wanted to trade their property in Burbank, for property out in the country. I went to go see what they had to offer. It looked just right to me! There was a nice two-bedroom house in front and small screen room bungalow in the rear. I could live in the smaller one and rent the larger one. That house would give me more rent than I was getting from the duplex we built. Since I had experience living in a duplex and renting out the other side, it seemed like a good move. The people from the Burbank property came out to see what I had to offer, and it turned out that it was just what *they* wanted. Surprisingly, we happened to both have the same bank for our mortgages. We told the bank that we wanted to trade places—each party assuming the mortgage of the other property, no money to exchange hands, trade property for property. I would leave all of the garden equipment, my stove, and a refrigerator, and they would leave a lawn mower, a hose, stove, and refrigerator. They would pay a mover to move them out of the Burbank house, and I would pay him to move me into it. Believe it or not, that is exactly what we did, and we were both content with the property swap.

Shortly after that, Graham came home from work and informed me that he was going to join the Marines. I was so proud of him and his decision to serve our country. But, I also realized that I was just a human being, like all of the other mothers whose sons enlisted into the armed services, and of course, who worry about the safety of their sons. *(Graham is pictured , his first official uniform photo.)*

Chapter 13

Burbank, California

Graham was sent to the Marine base in San Diego, California, for his boot camp training in 1942. Then he was sent east, to various places, and from there, to Pensacola, Florida, then to Camp Pendleton, then on to Cape Gloucester.

Kendra Blevins Ford

Mutual friends introduced me to Tom Tongate *(pictured below)* around this time. He was a widower who had two sons in the service: one in the Army, the other in the Navy. Neither of his sons nor Graham objected to our decision to getting married.

Unfortunately, the death of his wife was something to which Tom could not adjust. On top of this grief was the fact

They Said She Couldn't So She Did

that one of his sons was in the European conflict, the other in the Pacific. His son Bill was severely injured when caught between two army trucks at the Normandy beaches but recovered remarkably well. His other son, Jack, was hospitalized in San Diego for 11 months.

All of this was just too much for Tom to process. He wanted to live in Bakersfield; he spent nearly all of his time, off work, at the cemetery, visiting his late wife's grave. None of us could help him. One morning, he came to me and said, "I cannot stand to come home at night and not find Nellie May, (his deceased wife) here. You go your way, and I'll go mine. I want to live nearer to the cemetery."

Words cannot express how saddened I was to read about this brief, disappointing second marriage. So many questions remain surrounding this situation. Bernice saved just one photo of Tom. It is unclear how long they were actually married, but it appears to have been quite brief.

Well, I packed my things, and Tom helped move me back to the little house in Burbank. Then, I went down and tried to enlist in the Navy again, but was told that I was too old at age 46. I tried the Marines next and was turned down again. So I tried the army, and they took me!

Kendra Blevins Ford

Hearing these words for the first time literally made me gasp. I am right at the age of when she enlisted in the army and went to boot camp. I can't even imagine how tough it would be for a middle-aged woman in her 40s to go to boot camp! She had grit, indeed.

I had one week to get my things settled. Pauline, who lived in the front house of the duplex, agreed to collect the rent and deposit it in the bank for me while I was in the service. The bank arranged to keep the payments upon the property and make any necessary repairs on the place until I got out of the army. I was officially sworn in December 6, 1944. I left for boot camp on December 14, 1944 (which was my birthday), for Des Moines, Iowa. That was the strangest birthday I have ever had.

Our family was scattered across the globe during this time: Lucile was in Oregon, Damaris in New York, Graham in the South Pacific, Damaris' husband Peter on General Eisenhower's staff, and I was on a train going to boot camp. Not a single member of my family to speak to, or receive birthday greetings. And no birthday cake. I have had only one other birthday cake in my life since then.

Birthdays in my house are a reason to be celebrated. Everyone deserves to be recognized on their birthday. Don't wait until "next year" to celebrate your loved one's time around the sun. You just never know when

They Said She Couldn't So She Did

their time will be up. Had I known how important birthdays were to my great-grandmother, I would have made a greater effort to celebrate hers. During her final years, I was unaware of when her birthday actually was, or if anyone even acknowledged it, since I was just a teenager. This saddened me as I listened to the raw emotion in her recorded words.

There were two coaches of women going to Des Moines. The woman sitting next to me on the train was an attorney from Seattle. She was in the First World War as (I think it was called) a wren. We served in boot camp together, then at Percy Jones General Hospital in Battle Creek, Michigan, and then Fort Custer.

There were some really funny things that happened in boot camp. I was often dead tired—I had just turned 47 after all—and knew the girls who slept on either side of me were also tired. I told the girl on the right, and then the one left, "If I get to snoring, just say, 'Turn over, Mom, you're snoring', it won't wake me up, but I will turn over, and that'll be all there is to it." One night I was sleeping so soundly but was semi-conscious of giggling. I thought to myself, I wish those silly girls would shut up and go to sleep. Then, it got noisier, and a loud laugh woke me up. Everyone was standing around my bed, even the sergeant! Just laughing 'til their sides would split. The girl on the right said, "Turn over, Mom, you're snoring." I did. The girl on the left said, "Turn over, Mom, you're snoring." I did again. Everyone was having a high old time. I was flipping over on one side and then to the other, just like a fish out of water. Even the sergeant was giggling . . . and then she said, "Attention!" I sat up in bed.

At Percy Jones General Hospital in Battle Creek, Michigan, we often had to stand "convoy duty." Percy Jones was an amputation hospital at that time. Soldiers were flown from the battlefield with meager first aid treatment direct to Battle Creek. Our ambulances met the planes as they arrived. When the ambulances reached the hospital, the women were lined up two abreast. Upon the arrival of the ambulance, we moved up to it with our gurney, the medical crew lifted the patients from the ambulance onto our gurney, and then we rushed it into the auditorium, with a brief pause at every doctor station around the auditorium. We were told by the last station to transport the patient to a specific ward and a specific bed. Sometimes we were on the run for a long time, once or twice it was from midnight until ten or eleven in the morning! In which case we had an early lunch and then went straight to our regular duty. We called this "blood and mud" duty. Most of the soldiers were under sedation, which was just starting to wear off, so we had to actually run. It was a common thing in the PX to hear a bb shot, or shrapnel I suppose, drop on the floor. A soldier explained it to me, the first time I heard it. "Never look around to find out what dropped. Turn to the person sitting or standing nearest you and talk about something, and then laugh your fool head off." I thought the first time I was in the PX that they were just about the "laughingest" bunch I had ever seen. Now I know why.

From Battle Creek I was sent to Riverside, California, and from there to Camp Beetle, for my honorable discharge. While at Fort Custer, just a few miles from Battle Creek, I received a most peculiar message. We could never trace it or found out who sent it; it was from neither the Red Cross nor the army. The message was: "Cape Gloucester sunk. No survivors." My son Graham was on Cape Gloucester! We could not get verification in *any* way, and all I could do was pray that he would be found safe and sound. About three weeks later, I received a letter from Graham, and then more letters from him, but Graham didn't mention anything about the ship, so I didn't ask questions. I heard from other sources that some kind of a certain ship was selected as a target for sinking. Our intelligence department got wind of it and substituted a dummy ship in its place. The dummy ship *was* sunk, naturally without any survivors. I thought to myself, I must ask Graham about this and see if that is what really happened.

After my honorable discharge from the service, I received a letter from Graham stating that he would soon be coming home and sure enough, the next thing I heard, was his most welcome voice on the phone: "Hi, Mom! I'll be home this weekend."

Shortly after that, Graham and Virginia Lalowski were married. He was soon honorably discharged from the service as well. They lived in Los Angeles for a while, and then in Burbank. I worked in Van Nuys, at the veteran's hospital. In the due course of time, Paul arrived, my first grandchild. Then, along came my second grandchild, James. When James was only a few months old, Graham and Virginia decided to move to Chicago to live permanently. Eventually, Helene arrived, my first and only granddaughter.

All of my family were a long way off then, so very far away. Graham and his family were in Chicago, Damaris and Pete were in Alexandria, and Lucile was in Florence, Oregon.

Bernice's tone here indicates to me that she missed her family acutely. Graham's leaving for Chicago must have profoundly affected her since he was her only son, her entire world, for all of his growing up years.

Chapter 14

Redding, California

Bernice's Hymnal with her Redding Address

About this time, I was living in Burbank, California. The Birmingham Veteran's Hospital was waiting to be activated. I was selling Avon at the time to earn some extra money. So many people were being laid off during this time period, so my Avon sales were unfortunately going down, too.

Kendra Blevins Ford

I chuckled when I first read this, because it is yet another similarity between us as I, too, have sold Avon to make extra money!

I worked for a while at Advantage operating an electrical machine. It was precision work, which I liked, but the smog was getting so bad there, even while indoors, so much so that our eyes would water constantly. I just could not work with watery eyes. It so happened that my friend Stella wrote while I was still in Burbank and reported that they loved living in Redding and that there was no smog up there. They suggested I come up for a visit, and so I did. While up there, they suggested that since I was so far away from my family, I might as well be closer to them and also to my sister Lucile, so they encouraged me to move up to Redding. I found a nice place with a year's lease across the street from Paul and Stella. That rent could be applied to the purchase price of the property, and, after one year, if I liked it, I could apply to buy the house for myself. I did just that.

Shortly after the move to Redding, I went to work for Mercy Hospital. One day, we had quite an exciting afternoon and evening. The ranger station up at Mt. Glassman broadcast over the radio that all campers in that area were to leave immediately, as well as all property owners. It was feared that Mt. Glassman was going to erupt! Townspeople were told that all roads going into Mt. Glassman Park were closed. Only one-way traffic would be permitted. Well, I surely had a grandstand seat on my front porch to all of this. I was up high on a bluff and had an unobstructed view. I stayed up on my porch until 2:30 a.m. It turned out that there was only a slight discoloring of the sky. It did erupt in 1915, but the rumbling and trembling this time around were not as strong as back then.

When school would close for holidays or the summer, Lucile would come down and stay with me for a couple of days, or I'd go up and stay with her. Then, during Christmas vacation, she would stop overnight at my place on her way to spend Christmas with her son Juan, and then on her return, spend New Year's with me. We had many lovely drives along the coast and used to gather seashells, interesting rocks, and driftwood. I miss that a lot.

Redding had most of the advantages of a big city but had so much more to offer for recreation. Lucile encouraged me to try my hand at watercolor painting. It was hard for me to find the colors I wanted, but it was most interesting to mix my own. I had a lot of trouble painting things as they should be (in perspective). Impressionistic painting is not my strong suit. I do not think that I paint very well. A few of my paintings are not too bad, though.

Artistry tends to run in my family, on both my mother and my father's side. Perhaps many amateur artists feel similarly: not really good enough to paint to live, but love it enough to live to paint. I so wish I had one of my great-grandmother's paintings! I happen to enjoy painting myself, and try to stretch my creative side from time to time in this endeavor. That said, I don't think I paint very well, either.

One morning, I loaded my painting stuff in the car, made a hot bacon and egg sandwich, filled a thermos with hot coffee, and tossed in some fishing gear. I drove down to the Sacramento River. There was such a pretty, quiet place I had found. There was a small cove with a narrow strip of ground to walk on that led to a very small island. I went down very early in the day in order to get the sun rays and the reflections in the river and the small pond. I had to take several trips back and forth from the car to my private outdoor studio. I had just settled down with my breakfast when someone said, "What are you doing here?" He was a poor-looking individual; his clothes were ragged and torn. "I'm going to paint some pictures of the river." He told me to come to him and he would show me some beaver dams. I said, "Thanks, but I won't bother you or the beavers." I saw him

They Said She Couldn't So She Did

go across the little island. I had almost made up my mind to go home and forget about painting at all when two policemen appeared. They said they had seen my car and thought I had better not come to such a lonesome place so near the river. They asked if I was alone. I said that I thought I was alone, but a man just scared the wits half out of me and invited me to go see some beavers over on that little island. The policemen said, "We'll help you carry your things back to your car and maybe you should go on home." Well, I went home. I told some people about what happened at the river. They said an old hermit lives out that way and that I should be careful and not go out there anymore.

A couple of months after that, I woke up one morning and couldn't open my eyes. I dialed the operator and asked her to get my doctor. He called a cab to get me and take me to his office. I was told by the doctor that I had a very serious infection of the irises of my eyes. The intraocular pressure was extremely high; the doctor kept me at the office all day to monitor the pressure. He had several other doctors examine my eyes to confirm the diagnosis and his intended treatment. He informed me that if he couldn't get that pressure to drop, he would have to remove one eye. The medication was injected by a hypodermic needle into the eyeball. About 7 p.m., the pressure in my eye finally began to drop. My, what a relief. For three months I had to stay in a completely dark room. A neighbor helped me by preparing my food and shopping for me. I was able to listen to the radio and play my records, which gave some comfort, but I began to hate myself a little.

Long before I had this trouble in my eyes, I had my first airplane flight. I went back to Chicago to see Graham and his family. They had already been out here in Redding to visit me, and so I went out to visit them in Chicago for Mother's Day.

This plane trip was a very big deal for Bernice, she even had someone snap a photo of her prior to boarding the plane. As you can see in the picture on the following page, this is well before airport security was a thing to consider when traveling by air.

They Said She Couldn't So She Did

I had not met any of Virginia's family yet, beside her mother and father. They had a very nice, comfortable house, and a huge basement. There were cupboards with doors to put china in. When there was a big family gathering, everybody contributed, and they could have a big—and I mean big—gathering. They had enough dishes for 25 people! There was a double laundry tub set up so that it was easy to wash all those dishes. You won't believe this, but they had a jukebox. I never saw so many people in a private gathering have so much fun! We had enough food to feed an army. And believe you me, those people were wonderful cooks, every one of them!

During this visit, James, Paul, Helene, and I went downtown on the streetcar. We went to the museum, the zoo, and the natural history hall. During this trip, we went into a coal mine, learned how telephones operate, and saw lots of scientific things there were most interesting. Then we went to some of the big stores. I think I was there for five days, and I enjoyed it so much.

Now back to my story in Redding. There was a fine bowling alley not too far away from me in Redding. I enjoy bowling; however, league bowling is not for me. It's truly not. The tension is too much. For a while, I was bowling with a good friend and enjoyed it very much. One day I surprised both of us by getting one strike after another. I wasn't keeping score, but he sure was. I made a score of 200 one game and then 206 the next. Some people wanted to destroy me, which was frustrating to me. Someone was trying to "help" me by giving me the advice to do something else, and when I did follow that advice, I couldn't hit the side of a barn. One other lady made a remark, "There ain't no justice." I would have to agree.

They Said She Couldn't So She Did

Redding is a very hot place to live; in fact, temperature ranges of about 112-115 degrees is not uncommon there. Often, even with the air conditioning on, it's 100 degrees inside when I'm preparing supper.

I had a little sick spell while I lived in Redding. My doctor thought that the heat and the use of air conditioners were not helping my health. My doctor suggested that I get away from the extreme heat and move to the Bay area. Lucile had retired, and she and Juan had bought a house in that part of the country. They liked San Rafael and wanted me to come down that way. I was planning to go to Honolulu first, but then I would look into moving when I returned.

My plane left Redding about 11 a.m., and I had quite a wait at the San Francisco airport for my connecting flight to Honolulu. When we finally flew into Honolulu, we were met at the airport by a welcoming committee, with leis of beautiful flowers. The flowers were so fragrant!

I was part of a tour group, and we were taken all over the island to see interesting places. I was astonished to see how far the surfers took their boards out, it must have been at least a quarter mile. They could come in on the surf at such terrific speeds. It was fascinating to watch. I enjoyed seeing the pineapple fields, and people would happily pick fresh pineapple for you! They would put some salt on it, which made the fruit incredibly sweet!

Naturally, the flowers in Hawaii just captivated me, in color, size, and marvelous perfume. None of our flowers here on the mainland have quite the perfume the flowers in Hawaii had. Guava jam is delicious and oh, that guava ice cream, simply delightful. I hadn't experienced these things before, but they were both so good. We saw some beautiful ferns shown in the South Pacific. My, but it was heavenly there.

At the Kuna Inn, we had quite the scene. The hotel was right on the beach, and they had fine, wide sidewalks trimmed with beach and gardens. The waves rolled up on to the sidewalk! The desk clerk reassuringly said, "There's no danger; those are only 30-foot waves."

We drove to another side of the island. And it was just as lovely as could be. The food was marvelous everywhere we went. Oh, those orchid gardens were incredible. They even grow orchids in colors I had not seen before. I could hardly believe my eyes.

While I was having a fine time on this trip, Lucile had a lovely trip also to Rome, Florence, Athens, Madrid, and Lisbon.

They Said She Couldn't So She Did

Damaris was living in Spain at the time and Lucile visited her there. I was completely spoiled on this Hawaii trip. Every day my bed was made, and every night it was turned down. And woe is me, I have to do that for myself now. I think I'll just go back.

Lucile and I had a wonderful time swapping tales of what we did on our respected trips. After we were all talked out, I began to do some serious house hunting near San Rafael and the surrounding area. I was successful in finding a nice place in Catalina.

Chapter 15

Bay Area

I moved into the house in Catalina in the springtime. Ah, spring . . . it was nice to finally step outdoors and not get cold in half an hour! I suppose this sounds odd coming from someone living in California. Anyway, I discovered that it was peaceful and quiet there, too, which was refreshing. I had a small yard with a lawn in the front as well as the back, too, which had a fence around it to keep the stray dogs out. The biggest problem I needed to solve was how to get rid of the awful moles tunneling all over!

Moving to this peaceful area helped me want to take up painting again as a hobby, and my sister commented that I seemed to do better with it. I found that art was very relaxing for me and was a wonderful way to showcase my creativity.

Lucile and I saw each other about once a week since we lived near each other now. On these weekly visits, she often took me to San Francisco to try a different restaurant. One particular restaurant was unforgettable. It was called India House where we had the most interesting curry dinner. Oh my, it was wonderful.

Unfortunately, Graham's marriage to Virginia did not last, and they eventually divorced. Graham came back out to California to stay. Paul was in the Navy, James was working, and Helene was in high school.

For some reason, "New York life" just does not seem to go over very well here. I think the approach is wrong. All of the older people here are not so free to use given names and younger people almost never say "Mrs. So-and-so." That's one change we saw.

It is most evident here that Bernice felt strongly about using properly titled surnames when referring to one's elders. Since she did live in New York for a time, I imagine that this style of name usage was as appalling to her then as a New York resident as it was later in life when she returned to California, because of how she was reared.

Graham decided to change jobs and work at another insurance company. I hoped he would do well. His return to California included a return to dating other people. He eventually met someone named Donaldine that he was very much interested in, and before long, made plans to get married.

Kendra Blevins Ford

She already had a son named Rob, and a daughter named Cindy from a previous marriage. Graham and Donnie were married in a lovely home near San Rafael. They planned to drive back to Chicago in order to attend Helene's high school graduation. Paul was out of the Navy now, so Graham would get to see all three of his children on Father's Day while in Chicago. I stayed at their house and took care of their dog and cat and watered their plants and lawn. I could do that easily in the evenings. In the mornings I watered my lawn and plants and drove back and forth since it was not very far away.

There was a new style of living with teenagers and young adults. They were called hippies. And all I will say is, none of them are better than my people.

I find it interesting that Bernice brings up the subject of "hippies" from time to time in her story. Clearly, that era and those who followed the "hippie lifestyle" were quite distasteful to her.

One day, Lucile and I went to Napa. Lucile's grandson, Chuck, happened to be there for a visit. He liked to bowl, so I invited Chuck and Lucile to join me for lunch in Napa and then took Chuck bowling. I felt fine overall, but my vision was awful that day. When I made a spare, I could not tell which pins were still up because my vision was blurred. I told Lucile that I should probably stop bowling and go on back to my home in San Rafael. By the time I reached the house, I had a severe headache. So, I ate a light meal and went to bed.

Graham happened to phone me that evening, and his voice sounded very concerned that I didn't "sound right," and that he couldn't understand me very well, as my speech was a bit garbled, as if I was talking with a mouth full of food. I told him that I had gone to bed early, and had slept so hard that my arms and legs were still asleep and that my face felt like it was asleep also. This was not normal at all, but I didn't know any better. He told me to go see my doctor if I didn't feel okay the next morning. It turned out that I was having a stroke and didn't know it at the time. In the morning I was unable to move my left arm or my left leg, and the left side of my face was drawn out of shape, droopy-like. Knowing that these symptoms were definitely abnormal, I dialed the operator and told them to get a hold of my doctor and tell him to come over immediately. He came over right away and sent for Lucile to come and stay with me in my home for a few days. A few days later, I could walk very slowly, use my hands somewhat, and could talk a little. Shortly after that, we all talked it over and thought it would be better if I went to the veteran's hospital in Napa. I could get a room, have my meals served, and be close to medical health care if I needed it. There was a waiting list, so I found an apartment near Lucile in Napa and stayed there until I could be called to move into the veteran's hospital. Little by little I eliminated my furniture, dishes, and silverware because I would only have one room and would not need to cook, shop, or clean.

Well, I finally moved in to the veteran's hospital and things seemed very good at first, our meals were served on time, etc. It all just sounded "too good to be true." None of us could find a flaw anywhere, but now I know why. As soon as anyone had an ailment, phenobarbital was ordered by the doctor. "Keep them quiet and happy" was the motto there. Everyone eventually landed in the mental ward. My good friend, Amelia, is there now, actually. She doesn't know where she is, who she is, or who any of her friends are. When she gets ill, she calls her son instead and he takes her to her own doctor outside of the facility to take care of her.

On December. 14, 1969, Lucile gave me a lovely birthday party. Damaris came out for the celebration, traveling all the way from Alexandria, Virginia. My birthday falls so close to Christmas and that meant while growing up, I had to choose whether I would call my gift a birthday present or a Christmas present, but I never got both. That doesn't seem very fair, does it?

So, after a real feast, and a beautifully decorated and delicious birthday cake, all of them, one by one, presented a beautifully wrapped package to me. The first and largest gift I opened was a large suitcase. My first thought was, where will I put that? The second gift was a second suitcase, only a bit smaller, and then a third suitcase, and this time this case was a nice smaller size, one that seemed to be an ideal size for me, actually. But what will I *ever* do with those other two huge suitcases? I wondered. Graham could see that I was not only speechless but also a bit perplexed. They had wanted to surprise me. Well, they surely did! He said, "Open this other little one, Mom." And open it I surely did—it was crammed full of travel brochures featuring Alaska. (They knew I had always wanted to go to Alaska sometime in my life.) Graham said, "This is your birthday gift from all of us, Mom, and your Christmas gift is an all-expenses-paid trip for 30 days to Alaska. We thought it was time you had BOTH a birthday and a Christmas present, together in the same month." I just couldn't believe it. So many birthdays had been missed, overlooked, or downplayed. But not this year. I reveled in the joy of having my birthday acknowledged as well as having an actual Christmas gift and not having to choose between the two.

So, of course, Lucile and I had a marvelous time looking over all of those brochures and deciding how I wanted my trip to look, what tours to take, and creating an itinerary of a lifetime. Such good memories I have of this time we spent together like school girls laughing and dreaming of how it was going to be.

For some reason, I usually spent Thanksgiving with Graham and his family, and then spent Christmas with Lucile. This year, I spent both Thanksgiving and Christmas with my son Graham and my sister Lucile. I was to go over to Lucile's the day before Christmas, and she and I would get all the food preparation started. We would all gather together with both families on Christmas Day.

On December 24, I went to the dining hall for breakfast, the same as usual. When I returned to my room, I was told to phone my nephew urgently, but I had no idea why. He told me the grave news: Lucile had had a heart attack. Suddenly, all of the joyful Christmas plans were to be postponed to a later date. My nephew informed me that he would come to get me on Christmas Day and that we would go to the hospital and see Lucile. So we went to the hospital and I was immediately struck

They Said She Couldn't So She Did

at how *awfully* tired she looked to me, but that she didn't really look too sick. I was momentarily comforted by this and how she appeared to me.

I phoned Graham and told him about how she was doing and that she seemed to be doing okay, that she was "out of the woods" so to speak now that she was in the hospital. Graham talked with me and agreed that she'd be fine in a few days. We were wrong, however, so very wrong. Lucile's son Juan informed me the very next day that Lucile had died Christmas night.

I was beyond sad and upset, inconsolable, really. She and I were very close as sisters and had been our entire lives. We phoned each other literally every day. There was absolutely no communication barrier between us at all. To think that I could talk to her one day and know I would *never* hear her voice again, it did something to me. I just cannot explain how it is, words just escape me and the ones I do think of just don't convey the extreme sorrow I felt on the loss of my dear sister. Oh, how I wished I could come home from Alaska and tell her how wonderful my trip was. She always told me about her trips, and I was looking forward to doing the same for her. I would never get that chance.

Kendra Blevins Ford

After Lucile's death, I tried to keep myself busy in the occupational therapy department at the hospital. This was part of my prescribed therapy after my stroke and was helping me to be able to regain use of my weak left side and restore the strength it once had. Soon, however, it was time for my trip as the day of my departure to Alaska was fast approaching.

I had packed and re-packed my lovely suitcases so I would know just how much I could actually take. Knowing that you need to pack for a month-long trip, you need to pack a lot of stuff! The day before I was to leave, the evening news said that Greyhound Bus Line was out on strike! It so happened that I was to go by Greyhound bus the next morning to Seattle. Apparently, the bus from Seattle would not go anywhere beyond that, due to the strike. Well, that's no problem, I thought. Graham or Juan surely could take me from there. However, neither men were home to facilitate this transport for me! Now, what was I to do? I decided to pack my cases just as I had planned, and in the morning I went to the dining hall for breakfast as usual. When I returned to my room, I turned on the TV, and I learned that the strike was over. Phew! I was relieved to know that my arranged transportation was going to work out as originally planned. *(Graham wrote a tender not to his mom, Bernice, found in her Alaska travel journal on the next page.)*

They Said She Couldn't So She Did

Chapter 16

Alaska

Bernice took notes of her fantastic voyage to Alaska and entered them into this journal, pictured above. It was fascinating to read verbatim what she had spoken in her audio recordings. While some readers may feel there is too much detail in this chapter, preserving my great-grandmother's words was a priority during this writing, and therefore the details are maintained as they were recorded.

They Said She Couldn't So She Did

When the day of my long-awaited trip finally arrived, I was taken to the Greyhound bus station in time to catch my bus for Seattle at 1:50 p.m. The bus ride was overnight; I should have slept the whole way, but I was so excited for the commencement of my trip that I was awake for a good while. Eventually, I did succumb to sleep until our arrival in Seattle at 8 a.m. My initial plan was to get refreshed, eat a good breakfast and then go back to bed at the hotel I was staying, in order to get a little more sleep. But, wouldn't you know it, my hotel phone rang. I wondered who under the sun could be calling me. It was Graham! They wanted to see me while I was in Seattle, knowing I wasn't going anywhere until the following morning. He and Donnie were in Seattle also to hunt for a house to buy. He was going to be working in Seattle soon and so he was trying to get the housing piece figured out. They took me over to the property they had ultimately decided to buy, and then took me to breakfast. Apparently, they wouldn't be moving until the latter part of June when I had returned from my Alaskan trip. The next morning, I was to go by boat to Victoria, British Columbia, so I rested up in my hotel room after spending time with Graham and Donnie.

I had a lovely trip to Victoria. But no one seemed to know much about the islands we passed. I had a tour of the city, and also went to Butchart Gardens. I fondly recalled how I saw them back in 1924, and it was delightful to see how their dreams had materialized. No wonder they are a world attraction!

When we first landed in Victoria, I was taken by car to the Empress Hotel. Our luggage was put in one end of the lobby. When we returned from the tour, it was still piled up in the lobby. Some of us wondered if we should board the ocean liner for Alaska before supper or have supper here in the hotel. Absolutely no one could tell us, which was frustrating. The hotel clerks were clearly very unhappy about the 80+ people's luggage dumped in their lobby. I decided that I needed to have a good supper and didn't want to wait around in the lobby since no one had information about the evening meal. So, I went to the coffee shop and enjoyed a fine salmon dinner. A few moments after I came out of the coffee shop, there was an announcement over the PA system: all passengers going to Alaska traveling aboard the ship need to report immediately to a specific room.

We were given papers to fill out about emergency contacts, as well as other information, even though we had filled out all of this information previously. We were told that our ship could not enter the harbor due to some difficulties, as there were no Americans aboard the ship as part of the crew, which apparently was a big problem. We were told we could board a fishing boat to ferry out to the ship since the ship could not be docked where it would be easy for us to board. There were some people driving speed boats that circled around us numerous times, which was preventing us from getting on the fishing boat that would take us to the cruise ship.

Finally, the Coast Guard intervened and commanded the speed boats to leave the harbor. The fishing boat was finally able to pull up alongside the ship and we were all slowly helped aboard the ship. It was approximately 10:30 p.m. by this time, which meant we had been crammed on that fishing boat like sardines for about *two hours*!

Many trips were made back and forth to bring all of the booked passengers aboard the ship; it was *12:30 a.m.* when all passengers finally made it aboard. Thankfully, all of our luggage made it aboard, too. What a mess that would have been if our luggage had been left behind. Apparently, the ship crew was all non-American Greek origin, and not a single one of them spoke English, except for the captain. To say this made communication difficult is an understatement. We were guided to the dining room where we were treated to a scrumptious buffet, but we were almost ashamed to touch it! It was beautifully and artistically arranged and included hot soups, salads galore, cold baked ham, fried chicken, and so much more.

Next on the agenda was getting assigned to our staterooms. It was nearly *3 a.m.* before I could finally put myself into bed! I shall never forget the key they provided to me to secure my room. It was about as long as a ballpoint pen. It was very thick and heavy, with a Lucite tag having the name of the ship on it. Another interesting find was that the toilet paper came in a roll like wax paper, which I found rather amusing.

Our first port of call was Ketchikan, Alaska. Everyone was wondering what kind of a reception the ship would receive. Would we even be able to go ashore, given the issues we had just had leaving the evening before? The captain aboard the cruise ship didn't speak Greek and he had a devil of a time communicating to the rest of the crew that were trying to get that ship tied up to a dock.

We left Monday night from British Columbia and arrived at our port of call in Ketchikan on a Tuesday, about 7 p.m. *What a day it was*! We had beautiful, clear weather, and the passage was as smooth as a lake. And oh, the mountains were lovely!

As we approached the harbor, we could see crowds standing at the shore, waving a banner, but we couldn't make out what it said at first. As we drew closer, we saw that it read, "We are glad to have you come to Ketchikan!" I wondered to myself if they must have known all about the trouble we had in Victoria.

We had such a fine time touring the city of Ketchikan. The city was built in three elevations you might say, with huge terraces off the sides of the cliff. During the time of The 1964 Great Alaska Earthquake, rumor has it that most of the town slipped into the water; can you even imagine that? Sure enough, we could see a ship sunken in the harbor, and even a freight train with the train tracks twisted and hanging down from the land above it. The city of Ketchikan (so we were told) had the first street since that terrible earthquake, as well as the business sections, built upon two city block-wide cement docks anchored to the ocean floor. From there, one could climb a huge stairway, go up to the first row of houses, and then climb another set of stairs to reach the top terrace. Each stairway was at least a block long going up. The town was five miles long and three blocks high. It made for some interesting bus tour driving to say the least. We had to switch back and then back up to get the bus around the curve. The driver said, "Please join me in prayer as I make this turn!" We all cheered a hearty AMEN when he got straightened out. I can't even imagine what they do when it snows.

We had four hours to sightsee and shop that day. We left Ketchikan at 11 p.m., and the sun was just starting to set! When we returned to the ship, we had a beautiful buffet supper and were treated to some of the most graceful dancing I've ever seen.

Unfortunately, it was a really rough night of sailing as we headed onward to our next port of call. I felt miserable all night. I was too sick to go eat in the morning, in fact, only a few other passengers made it to breakfast. By mid-morning, things had smoothed out and I was up and about and had a fine lunch. The food was excellent on the ship!

We were due to arrive at Juneau, the next port, at 7 p.m. The captain had a tough time with such a large ship in a small harbor, and boy, did he get angry! At last, he began to signal with his right hand, shouting and swearing at the crew who only understood Greek. It took nearly an hour to dock the ship so that we could begin sightseeing.

My, but Juneau was gorgeous! The glacier and that charming chapel by the lake were some of the best scenes from that particular port of call. We turned in early, as we were informed that we would be called at 5:30 a.m. for an inspection!

They Said She Couldn't So She Did

The traveler company representatives didn't know any more about it than we did and they were nervous wrecks about this "inspection." Some of the passengers who had traveled a lot helped them get untangled from the red tape and the inspection. In Juneau, we would be disembarking temporarily from the cruise ship and staying at a hotel in the city called the Klondike hotel.

We had to wait a bit for our room assignments at the hotel, but they kept us happy with coffee and coffee cake, then had our luggage delivered to our rooms. My room had a queen-sized bed, which was pretty big for just me. There were beautiful, heavy drapes over the large picture windows to keep out the midnight sun, thank goodness. The furniture was lovely and tasteful, and there was even free instant coffee in my room. At night, my bed was turned down and the view from my room was absolutely breathtaking: it had the most majestic mountain view, with snow piled up high on the mountaintop, yet no snow on the ground level.

I decided to freshen up a bit, and then I went downstairs to go do some sightseeing. I was eager to see what the town looked like. Oh, the shops! The stores had such beautiful things in them. There was one particular store that I wanted to visit, as the window displays were just magical. But unfortunately that particular store wasn't open yet, so I decided to have lunch in the meantime and then went back again to see if it was open for business. But it still wasn't open.

Frustrated, I stepped into the shop next door to inquire as to when it might open up for business. Out of the blue, a person approached me tentatively and I was racking my brain as to how or why I should know this person. She said, "I feel like I ought to know you. Where are you from?" In a few moments her husband came into the room and cleared the hesitation we felt by saying, "Well, Bernice, what a surprise to see you here!" This man had owned the store in Redding where I had bought my furniture some time ago and now lived here in Alaska. What a fun encounter and a nice little visit we had. Then he informed the owner of the store next door that a friend of theirs had just come in and inquired as to when the shop would be open. The owners of the store I really wanted to visit came right down and let me shop in their store. I wanted to buy a genuine fur rug. Someone on the cruise ship had said that this particular shop had top quality furs. After browsing the store carefully, I chose and bought a small yet beautiful fawn rug. Happy with my purchase, I moved on to another store and was delighted to find a miniature dog sled and an igloo, which I just had to have as a souvenir from this trip. Lastly, in one of the final stores I browsed, I bought myself a lucky jade and amethyst brooch and bracelet; they were breathtakingly beautiful.

The mountains visible from Juneau looked as if they had stood in the water of the bay for ages and reached, it seemed, to the sky. There were no beaches present.

Meals were less expensive than I thought they would be in Alaska. I had venison, mashed potatoes, slaw, blackberry pie, and coffee. They were very large servings and oh so delicious.

At the museum, we saw some beautiful things; the most beautiful (I thought) was a patchwork quilt made of tiny feathers from the necks of ducks. There were different color combinations for different squares, and it was kept in a glass case. The maker of the quilt was over 100 years old and had just passed away a few days ago prior to the time of my visit. On the back of the quilt, she had sewn tiny bags of peppercorn to every other square to preserve it and protect it from pests.

It had been a beautiful sunny day in Alaska, and surprisingly, the temperature was only 60 degrees! Having gotten up so early, I had a light supper and decided to turn in early. We would leave for Whitehorse the next day, and I didn't want to miss a thing. The mountains there were so unbelievably high. I took a train tour while in Juneau. The train was wonderful; down both sides of the train, there were two rows of swivel chairs in a staggered pattern. This way everyone can turn quickly around and see what the others are so excited about. The people next to me had traveled extensively, and they were as thrilled as I was at the majestic scenery around us. We wondered how anyone could have crossed these mountains or survived the extremes.

We left Skagway at 10 a.m. and had lunch at a restaurant called Luke Bennet. We were told it would be caribou stew. If it was, it was as delicious as old-fashioned, homemade stew with potatoes, carrots, onions, and plenty of gravy; we ate it with hot biscuits followed by apple pie and coffee.

We arrived at Whitehorse at about 4 p.m. I was tired and a bit carsick from the many turns on our trip. Others were a bit queasy also. The hotel at Whitehorse was spic and span new! The paint was so fresh, you could still smell it. My, it was spacious and beautifully furnished. A group of us went to a museum and did some shopping. Then we had supper together. One of the women lived in Seattle, and the other in Vancouver, Washington. We enjoyed being in a small group. All of us were tired, and in a short time, one could walk all over town. None of us were interested in nightlife, and knowing we would leave early in the morning, we all turned in early.

For the next part of our trip, we would go by bus to Fairbanks. The bus driver told us that we would most likely see wild animals en route to our destination. As we spotted wild animals, we were told to "point" to the animals according to the numbers on a clock, so that others could turn and have a chance to see what was in view. The driver stated that, if able, he would pull to the side of the road a bit for longer viewing. We saw eagle nests in some of the trees, and quite a few of the wild mountain sheep (the curly horned ones). At one point, someone called out, "one o'clock!" and to the right of the road, we could see the high brush moving, and then we saw the huge antlers of a moose. The driver attempted to open the door so that we could get a good picture of it, but the moose was frightened by the motion and quietly walked into a small lake.

The scenery in Fairbanks was absolutely magnificent; it is really hard to put it into words that can describe the beauty, and the weather was just ideal for sightseeing.

We stopped at Alice Khan Border Lodge and stayed overnight. We had very good accommodations there, but unfortunately, there really wasn't much to see while there.

However, the room was fine and the food superb. We had traveled over 250 miles that particular day and boy, were we glad to have a change of pace.

We were to leave the lodge at 8:30 a.m. I got up early to have a short walk before breakfast, and almost wished I had not! I saw a new building being put up a little ways off. So, being a fairly brave person, I decided to walk down and see what it was. I found out it was being guarded by two of the most fiendish huskies I *ever saw*! They were growling, barking, and baring their teeth at me. I was afraid to take my eyes off of them, and so I backed up as fast as I could. But they had their eyes on me now and so they followed me. A ranger at the station just happened to see me from the window and yelled at them to "Sit!" Thank goodness they obeyed their master. I was pretty scared during this dog encounter. I know now that those dogs were only doing their duty, but they didn't know that I was only looking and meant them no harm.

I was told by folks in Alaska that "Ph.D." stood for "post hole digger." Some houses, which had been built on permafrost/frozen ground, yet kept cozy warm by the occupants, began to sink over time due to the temperature difference. The army engineers in the service of Alaska soon discovered that the covered ground actually *melted* and that it was now necessary to put in a refrigeration system in the foundation of the buildings to keep them from sinking. Construction, therefore, was extremely expensive there in Alaska, even back when I visited. We were told one newcomer had wanted to dig a well. Not only would he have to dig down 800 feet, but it would also cost him $15 per foot!

The next day's Alaskan adventures would start very early. We were headed to Newcomb territory and needed to have our bags packed and be checked out of our hotel rooms. We had a very long ride ahead of us, about 315 miles, and would arrive in Fairbanks at about 6 p.m.

What impressed me most of all regarding the scenery in Alaska is that there was only snow on the top of the mountains. One of the most beautiful sites was where part of a huge snowbank had melted away, and appeared as if someone had poured old-fashioned bluing on it. Another surprising thing: although we were not at a very high altitude, the trees were tiny and not tall at all.

Our first stop in Fairbanks was at the hotel, to get our luggage placed and to get us settled in. Just as you approached the massive door, one would behold a breathtaking fountain of soapstone dolphins leaping around in the water. It looked so incredibly real, I was almost tempted to stay back to avoid being splashed! Oh, it was quite fascinating, even mesmerizing to look upon.

Inside the foyer of the hotel was an immense picture of a giant polar bear. Everything within the hotel was richly decorated in red, black, and gold. I had a delicious supper while at the hotel—Swiss steak. One of my activities while at this hotel was a paddleboat ride on an old river steamer that cruised up a river.

The hostess at the hotel was an authentic Alaskan native of Point Barrel. She was particularly friendly to me and promised to bring me a sample of moose, elk, and whale from her home. I told her that I had originally planned to eat local, native food just as the residents of each city I visited, but found zero local fare on the restaurant menus, which was vastly disappointing. The hostess explained to me that each harvest of meat was divided by the hunter to his entire family, as many kin as they can. The hostess' folks sent her an allowance of fish and meat from time to time. When she offered to bring me some of this, I insisted that it be small—just the size of a matchbook cover, enough for a taste, really, not a full meal.

They Said She Couldn't So She Did

The school building in Fairbanks was rather unique, large enough to contain a basketball court as well as a football field! It was completely circular and fully enclosed. There were only two outside doors to this vast building. There were administrative offices, school rooms, cafeteria, and laboratories on one end, while there were the athletic facilities—including a gym, locker rooms, and additional athletic fields—on the other end, all inside. All doors on the beams were firmly on the inside of the circle, with everything facing the center. This specialized design helps keep the frigid sub-zero cold out, a norm in Alaska of course. Out in the parking lot, which somewhat looked like a vintage outdoor theater, there were gadgets you park next to within the parking lot system. These gadgets came with a long electric cord that plugged into your car to keep it warm; it also kept the battery charged.

I marveled that the sun would set at 11 p.m. and rise at 3 a.m.! Now that's a short night. I would think that would take some getting used to. I hope being a state now will not change it as statehood has changed Hawaii. The people in Alaska are such wholesome individuals, no make-believe there. You either like them or you leave them alone. I was sorry to leave. Oh, I forgot to tell you: there was a Sears Roebuck & Co. Store, gasoline stations, a very nice modern beauty salon, a laundromat, and even a Sizzler restaurant. Signs on the doors said, "No shoes, no shirt, no service." They just turned the hippies out everywhere, thank goodness. I had my hair done while in Alaska and my "shampoo and set" was just $6.50.

We left Fairbanks by airplane for Anchorage. Anchorage is a much larger city, has neon signs, traffic signals, and sadly, a lot of hippies. Elsewhere we felt free to walk at 11 p.m. at night, but I did not feel safe to do so here. I took a taxi to a place that was very highly praised as a place to go for good King salmon. I also got a salad, baked potato with sour cream, and coffee for just $4.95, which was not bad!

We left Anchorage for Kotzebue, then flew to Nome and transferred to a smaller plane. At the airport, we were ushered into a huge room with row upon row of racks of heavy coats upon us. We were told to wear whatever coat we wanted up to Kotzebue, where we would go beyond the Arctic Circle. The snow was absent at Nome and Kotzebue. I had expected to see tons of snow and even have a ride on a dog sled! The houses in Kotzebue appear like shacks, but many of them actually have good furniture in them. Building is much too expensive there, given the severe weather conditions, and no food is wasted. What is not edible is thrown out and the high tide washes it out to sea. A memorable meal I had there was a reindeer steak, which was very tender and good, accompanied by soup, salad, coffee, and ice cream. All for $5.50! A New York steak was $7. I bet it never came off the beef here since the reindeer are much more plentiful!

The Eskimo dancers I observed while in Alaska mostly used movement of the hands and were very graceful, dancing to lots of drumbeats, but not musical at all. To see the dancing once was enough for me. I enjoyed viewing the wonderful ivory carvings so much more than the dancers. One of the native Alaskan men I met was a local painter. He was quite friendly and had beautiful eyes and skin. For living in such a barren, frigid, and desolate place, the people were rather jolly there and seemed to enjoy their lives. I was attracted to the lovely and very expensive furs for sale in the shops in town (even though I had already purchased one), but was also captivated by the lovely baskets made of the inside of a baleen whales' mouth. If you didn't know, the baleen whale screens food through its mouth, the membrane of which is as large as horsehair. This material was woven to form baskets, which made for incredibly beautiful workmanship.

Kendra Blevins Ford

On the flight, I had a most delicious and memorable drink called a black Russian: it included vodka, coffee, and special spices and was poured over ice. The Alaskan people were quite charming. If I was much younger I'd seriously consider a move to Alaska. Unfortunately, I am too old now to stand the extreme change in the climate. They have street lights there, but even at 3 a.m. they do not dim at all. I did experience a very slight earthquake during my visit to Alaska, but I hope that is the last one. From what I've seen, it's unthinkable to endure a full-fledged earthquake there. It is wondrous to observe how everything grows so wonderful there, with this lovely peat moss everywhere, as plentiful as our dry soil in the lower 48.

On the morning we began the first leg of the return trip home, I had a delightful late coffee break about 11 and just relaxed and enjoyed the beautiful scenery here in Alaska, knowing that my time here was shortening rapidly. We arrived in Seward right in time for lunch. There was not much to see in this town and I wasn't feeling too well as I seem to have caught a cold. I decided to just go aboard and rest in my stateroom. Oddly, I had to ask for a different stateroom, as the floor was soaking wet in my first assigned room and was not fit for occupancy. This ship's crew was lacking in niceties and the food quality was considerably less ostentatious than what we had at the beginning of our trip. We stopped at the towns of Sitka and also Cordova, but feeling great fatigue from my ill-timed head cold, I decided to just hang out on the ship. I quickly found a sheltered, sunny place to sit out on the deck and remained there for the greater part of the day. I was treated to a magnificent view of the glaciers, and I saw yet again some twisted train tracks with a half of a submerged freight train just like I did in Seward. It was a rather troubling sight, actually, when you think about what happened during that earthquake. Many of my fellow passengers stayed on board as I did, enjoying the majestic mountain view that lacked commercialization. It's God's unsurpassed handiwork, indeed.

During a part of this cruise, the water was very rough, and so I didn't attend the captain's celebration party, an apparent highlight of the trip filled with lavish food choices and entertainment. My hearing was muffled from the head cold and the swaying of the anchors near my stateroom caused me all kinds of vertigo-related grief, while I was still dealing with a rather bothersome cough. I was glad to be promised calmer waters and fabulous scenes at Glacier National Park for the next day. We took a pilot on board to help locate icebergs then. There is something to be said about that gorgeous blue ice we saw there! We've been made aware that we may see some polar bears on the icebergs and to watch for them. The snow on the glaciers is actually not "snow white" as one might assume; instead, it's rather dirty looking and brownish, reportedly from the mountainside surface dust scraped by glaciers.

I did end up going ashore at Sitka as it was a beautiful sunny day, and there we saw some more evidence of the earthquake. I found it rather interesting to see that Sitka is surrounded by many small islands. Another bizarre piece of trivia to share is why candlefish are so tall. Apparently, they are an extremely oily fish. After harvest they are hung up to dry thoroughly; native Alaskans can then light them like a candle. Although they don't give near as much light as a candle, they burn slowly and last longer.

On one of the final days of my return trip, I had a fun surprise happen to me. I had just entered my cabin when suddenly, there was a knock at the door. Lo and behold, but a crew member had a package for me! What a delightful surprise it was, a lovely gift-wrapped box of See's candy from my son Graham. What a thoughtful, lovely way to say that he was looking forward to my return home.

Glacier National park was everything I thought it would be: waterfalls galore and icebergs floating all over the place. I learned that when a small iceberg breaks off of a larger one, it is called calving. I've seen so much beauty and majesty here made by nature that I'm simply overwhelmed by the beauty. But soon I will have to live surrounded by the dull manmade stuff. This Alaskan trip has been everything that I had dreamed it would be, but the beauty and majesty were more than I ever could have imagined. I started to feel better from my head cold, so attended the farewell party for our ship's Admiral, which was so much fun. When I arrived in Seattle, I stayed with some friends and then made the final journey back home. Although incredibly worn out, I was so very glad I took this trip and am forever grateful that my family gave it to me.

Unfortunately, in my quest for pictures and memorabilia, I was not able to find any pictures from the Alaska trip or any souvenirs from the experience.

Chapter 17

Seattle

Although the quality of the above photo is not optimal, I decided to include it because you just can't miss the smile on Bernice's face as she poses with my brother and me during our first visit with her in Seattle.

I just could not stand to stay in the facility at Yountville any longer. I am still convinced to this day that far too many so-called "pain easers" were being issued to residents just to keep them from complaining. I truly believe they were dishing out phenobarbital to everyone. No one wanted to get involved in resolving this concern of mine; they simply did not want to hear about it.

At one point when I became quite ill and was taken to the hospital one particular Sunday night, the nurse on duty at the time was rather irritated to be called to help me. I didn't even see the doctor, but I think that I should have since I had severe nausea and diarrhea. She told the ambulance driver who was to transport me, "Take her back." To me, she said (and I remember, as I told her this was *diarrhea* I had), "If you do this again, I'll put you in the hospital for keeps!" What kind of nurse treats a person like that, as if I were making up my symptoms and creating problems for her on purpose. As soon as I was able, I phoned my son Graham and asked if I could come up and stay with him until I could find a suitable apartment since the place I was currently at was making me most unhappy.

Graham had a beautiful three-level home in Seattle around this time. If you went in by way of the carport, you walked into the dining area and the kitchen. If you entered from the front door, you went into the vestibule with a stairway going up and another going down. In the hall were two bedrooms and a bath for Rob and Cindy. The living room was vast and magnificent. I believe the ceiling was 16-18 feet high, with a fine fireplace that was arranged in such a way that each floor had access to it, meaning each room had a fireplace, also! Upstairs was a master bedroom, with only a half wall on the living room side, giving it the appearance of a mezzanine balcony, and anyone could look over the edge and see what is going on down below. Downstairs from this level was the big family room with a TV, bar, pool table, piano, comfy furniture, and sliding doors that led out to the back yard. Near this was a large laundry room, and then down the hall, there was a lovely large room that served as my living room and bedroom with an adjacent bath complete with tub and shower. Graham and Donnie had a gorgeous deep red velvety calceolaria in my living space; it was a dramatic beauty. Being in this home made me feel like I was miles away from the city, as there were evergreen trees all around the property. I wished I could walk all over the property; unfortunately, there were no sidewalks. There were ditches on each side of the street, but no place for me to go to get out of the way of cars, and in the rain, I thought I might zig where I should have zagged!

    I moved to a place called Ballard. My health had declined and my strength had decreased, causing me to fall frequently. My grandson James and his wife Ginny lived nearby. I believe he

They Said She Couldn't So She Did

worked in management for McDonald's. Sadly, I did not see them very often. Donnie's kids were living on their own now; I usually saw them on Thanksgiving or Christmas.

I am so proud of my granddaughter Helene. She is a girl to be very proud of. She worked full time and went to school, and that is no fun. Believe me, I have done it and I know. She studied to be an inhalation therapist. That meant 365 days for three years to finish the course. When someone works *that hard* to learn how to help someone who is not as fortunate, someone they do not know, you better believe me, they deserve nothing but praise. She is my granddaughter, and I am *so proud* of her accomplishments.

About this time, we were looking forward to having a visit with my grandson Paul, his wife Kathy, and their two children, Kendra and Ian. Graham planned to meet them at the airport and then take them to Lake Cushman for a few days. From there Graham planned to take them to Port Angeles, where they can experience sleeping on Graham's new yacht, and then they will come up to visit me. Paul and Kathy are my grandchildren; Kendra and Ian are my great-grandchildren.

I thought, since all of the grownups had been entertained so nicely, and this would be my *first time* to see them (and could be my last), I would like to keep it in reach of the kids, as far as entertainment goes. We had a picnic at Woodland Park and the kids rode on everything that walked, except an elephant, a giraffe, and a camel, you might say. I honestly believe watching the kids was more fun than I'd had for a long time. Oh, what dear little faces; they just glistened. They could only stay a couple of nights, and then Graham took them to the airport to fly back home.

I so wish I could recall in rich detail when this visit happened, but I was just 5 years old at the time. I do recall the airplane ride to Seattle and some bits and pieces of the visit. The pictures are evidence of a good time had by all, given the smiles on everyone's faces. In the following picture, she must have been saying something to us as both my brother Ian and I seem to be listening to her while the picture was taken. From left to right: Graham Blevins, Kendra Blevins, Bernice Tongate, Ian Blevins, Paul Blevins

They Said She Couldn't So She Did

Kendra Blevins Ford

My younger sister Damaris worked with the Smithsonian Institute as well as National Geographic; she's traveled all over the world as a co-hostess. She's even had the opportunity to travel to Iran, Pakistan, Afghanistan, and part of Russia. One year after we lost Lucile she took time out of her busy career to come over to the west coast and visit with me.

While looking through an old box of memories that had been part of Bernice's estate, I found several postcards sent by Demaris to Bernice that prove that she did indeed travel to many international destinations.

In preparation for her upcoming visit, Graham helped me finance a trip to the Big Island. I had already taken her to see the most interesting places she had wanted to see in Seattle on prior visits. This trip to the Big Island, I thought, would be both unique and fun for the two of us, but it was not much of a success. In fact, I thought it was rather anticlimactic. The time of her visit had come to an end and so I bid her farewell as she resumed her world travels as part of her career. Her next trips included destinations such as Cambodia, Hong Kong, Manila, Malaya, but then abruptly canceled out on the rest of the trip and didn't go to Japan as originally planned.

She came up to Seattle to visit with me instead. This time, I took her over to Victoria, a part of the country she had never seen. We went to the Empress Hotel and participated in a formal tea. We saw the museum, the parliament buildings, and then one evening we returned to the Empress Hotel for a lovely dinner. But this visit just felt like we were going through the motions. I just couldn't shake the feeling that something was wrong with her; I didn't know what was wrong, but she just seemed "off." The sightseeing we experienced together seemed to bore her, and she didn't seem like herself, either. I later told Graham that I would not ask Damaris back out to visit with me again. He reflected on everything I said about our visit and commented that she seemed like a very frustrated person. During her visit with me, I was surprised to see her drink so much, literally at every opportunity that presented itself, so much so that it worried me.

One day I had a letter from her that I could hardly read, the lines went every which way, some letters were huge, and I began to wonder if her lack of interest in the trips to the West Coast was due to some strange illness that was affecting her. I telephoned her out of concern, and she said, "No, nothing's wrong, I'm just fine, just fine." But she didn't sound fine at all to me. She was a great believer in the power of positive thinking and almost seemed to live in an alternate reality. I believe that if someone cannot admit that they are ill, it becomes a case of not being truthful because you are hiding the truth. Even Lucile didn't tell either of us that she had a heart problem. It is unfair to those nearest to you to joke, poke fun of, or mislead people as to your true physical well-being. She insisted that there was nothing wrong with her, and yet revealed to me in her letter that she broke down and cried on the airplane after she left to return home after her visit with me. In this letter, she also told me that she had a condition of the eyes called deterioration of the macula. Her doctor had informed her that no one knew what caused this degenerative eye condition and that there was no known cure for it.

I called her on the phone and implored her to come and live with me and not try to live on her own anymore, but she would not relent. My poor health and all of its associated troubles (as I had had another recent stroke) prevented me from traveling out east as I just couldn't risk a fall. I knew my limitations and felt that a long plane ride would just be too much for me to handle. Virginia's winters were far different than what I was accustomed to in California. I was also having problems walking and knew that I would not be able to walk on ice and snow safely.

They Said She Couldn't So She Did

A few weeks after my telephone conversation with her, I learned that she was admitted to a hospital for an unknown illness from which she did not recover. Sadly, she died on December 9, 1974. I was unable to go back east to attend the funeral, which was almost more than I could emotionally bear. I suddenly realized that I was the only one of Mama and Papa's children that were left. I missed both Lucile and Damaris with my whole heart.

Talking about illness and death makes a person feel sad, doesn't it? Although I have my own challenges with health, some people struggle with things that many of us take for granted, like being able to hear. I am grateful that my ears still work well enough and that I can understand people when they speak to me. I can only imagine the challenges and struggles that a person who cannot hear would face.

One day, though, I had a chance to see firsthand how hard it could be for a deaf person to do something as normal as going shopping. While I was checking out at a local grocery store, I saw a lady who could neither speak nor hear words that were spoken to her. The lady and the sales clerk were exchanging notes and it was evident that they were both getting upset with one another because it was taking so long to achieve understanding. I myself was getting a little upset waiting for both of them to complete the checkout process. I stepped up and told the clerk if she would give me a pen and a pad of paper, I would stay with this lady until she found what she needed.

On my way home on the bus, I wondered how many other people needed help as she did. But I wondered to myself, how could *I* help them? Soon two women boarded the bus and sat across the aisle from me. I was fascinated watching them communicate with each other so quickly and yet so easily with their hands. They appeared to be having so much fun; the smiles on their faces and their bright-eyed expressions shone so brightly to me. I *knew* that was the answer: I *had* to learn sign language! I spent half a day trying to find out where a person could get lessons to learn sign language. Finally, I was directed to where I should go. I went to the place and simply explained that I wanted to learn sign language so that I could help someone while shopping, and visit them in nursing homes or while they were in a hospital. I was given an extremely long form to fill out, and then I was directed to go next door where someone could help me. One of the women in the office told me to follow her, and so I did. But then she began to give me the third degree: where was I born, when, where did I live, what was my Social Security number, my phone number. So far so good. How much

They Said She Couldn't So She Did

education did I have, did I have a savings account and how much? What? That seemed to be rather irrelevant for a sign language class! I responded to this woman's query by asking her, "Do you have you a savings account and how much would there be in it? I'm a person that likely feels just the same way you do, and I'm asking relevant questions such as: do you teach sign language here, what time do the lessons start, where are they held, how much do the lessons cost, and how much is the instruction book! None of the other questions are important, and you ought never to ask such personal questions, in my opinion. Please understand I know that it is not your fault, but it is not anyone's business at this school." If the schools taught lessons instead of prying into an individual's personal affairs, maybe taxpayers would vote for their school bonds. But now, I know better.

At just that moment, one of the other women came into the room and said that I was exactly right. Then she added, "I may know someone who lives near you, who could teach you sign language privately. I will try to find someone close to you; if you will give me your address and phone number, I will share it with them." She phoned someone and sure enough, I only had to walk about ten blocks once a week to start learning sign language! Eventually, I found out that there are many different styles of sign language, just as we hear people with various accents, expressions, and slang. What a pity that it wasn't a more universal language. I sure hope Braille is. I did learn sign language well enough to want to teach it to others, and soon sought opportunities to do just that.

    I went to the senior citizen's housing authority and asked if they had residents who were deaf and if so, would any of the hearing residents like to learn sign language for free so that they could communicate with residents who couldn't hear. At last, I was able to get a class started at the Franklin Apartments on Rainer Avenue. To get to this building, I had to take a bus, transfer to another bus, arrive at my location, and teach from 9:30 until 11. Then I would return home, snatch a bite to eat, and then go to the Northwest Senior Citizen Center in Ballard and teach a large class of 15 people. I enjoyed teaching this sign language class so much, and my students did also. In fact, when I moved from the area, three of my sign language students came to see me. I had another bad stroke and subsequent fall. This put a stop to my current pursuits and I had to give up teaching sign language. I could not get on and off the buses independently, nor could I walk very far. This was very hard for me to accept, but I had no other choice but to do what was best for my health and safety.

They Said She Couldn't So She Did

This new setback in regard to my health meant I needed to consider the best place to live that would be close to my son, Graham. Around this time, Graham and Donnie bought a yacht and started to live on it. He had been transferred to Port Angeles and was given a very large transfer bonus to go from Tacoma to Forks. While contemplating this, I soon realized that it would be quite a trip if I needed him, and in order for them to come to help me, it would take them a long time to get to me. They would have to come farther by boat. And since they would need to travel by boat, one must consider the fact that boats do not travel as fast or as frequently as the buses run. Graham and Donnie looked around for an apartment near their docked houseboat. Port Angeles is small and hilly, which might be more trouble than it was worth, and so they looked over in Sequim, which turned out to be nice as it has less rain and is actually warmer than Port Angeles. I decided to take that apartment in Sequim; it sounded like a very nice place to live that was not too far from the grocery and general merchandise stores.

Chapter 18

Sequim

The apartment in Sequim was lovely with lots of light, a very large living room, two bedrooms, kitchen, dining area, and a cute little patio. It was about a full two-block walk to the store, six blocks to the post office, and eight blocks to the library. It seems like each place was measured in miles instead of blocks. In Ballard, it was difficult to walk even one long block, but it was also very windy there. I soon found out that one round trip to the store was my limit; I just didn't have the strength or the stamina to go farther than that. To help me with my walking, I bought a dandy four-wheeled grocery cart at Sears with a plastic liner and cover. That kept my groceries dry when it rained and also gave me much better support than trying to walk with a cane while carrying a bag of groceries for several blocks.

My goodness, but it was so wonderful to get outside and walk in the fresh air! The mornings were the best time to walk because there tended to be a brisk breeze blowing in the afternoon, which made me feel chilled. There were two good

They Said She Couldn't So She Did

shops for me to choose from here. One was Southwood's Grocery, and just across the street from it was the Town and Country shopping center. I did most of my shopping at Southwood's. It was a general mercantile-type store, and they carried just about everything. Town and Country had reasonable clothing for sale and I had good luck finding slacks and blouses that suit me there. At first, the air seemed cold to me when I first moved to the area, but it could have been my poor circulation that affected my perception of temperature.

On one particular day, I had my mind made up and I wanted to find some union suits. I was frustrated to learn that I couldn't find union suits at either of the stores near me. I phoned J.C. Penney's in Port Angeles regarding the inquiry whether or not they carried union suits, and the following conversation actually took place: "Do you have ladies' union suits?" "What?" "Union suits." "No, I don't think so. What union is it?" Exasperated, I then rephrased my query, "Do you have long johns?" "Yes." Finally, I was getting somewhere. "Do you have any ladylike long johns?" "No." Do you see why I say Sequim is such a quaint little place? Where else would you have such a conversation? I then went to the Sears mail order store and they had them! So I ordered three union suits and got them delivered in three days from Seattle.

Kendra Blevins Ford

Another "great" thing about Sequim . . . to mail a letter to my son Graham, it had to go clear over to Tacoma, then by a mail truck, then come back through Sequim on its way to Port Angeles. No wonder we had such a dumb postal service with rates that go up 15 cents!

I decided that this was *the year* I would go to a class offered by the local community college. Since the back taxes were held here in Sequim, the tuition was one dollar for instructions on how to do some writing. Lucile had often said that since I had so many unusual things happen throughout my life, that I ought to write them up and publish my story.

Well, we had 10 senior citizens in my class, and we met once a week. The teacher made a copy of each student's handwritten lessons even though we had to read our papers out loud to the entire class. This was a tremendous waste of taxpayer's money, in my opinion. Some of us wrote six, eight, or even 10 pages! Now run off ten copies like that and see how much paper you use up. One of the students made the comment, "Isn't this a waste of paper?" She was told, "Oh no, no, no, you don't pay for it, so don't worry about it, doesn't cost us anything." No wonder our schools do not have enough money! I don't think I learned very much about autobiography writing in that class. But I'll admit that I wasn't taught much despite taking the course.

One of the women in the writing class was astounded and mesmerized with the idea of women enlisting in the Navy. Well, I kindly explained that this actually happened in 1917, because not only did I write about it, *I did it*. Now here it is 60 some odd years later and people are hearing about women enlisting for the very first time. A woman in my class asked me if I would allow a journalist friend of hers to write it up for the 4th of July edition of the local paper. I consented, thinking it sounded pretty benign to do. Now, I wholeheartedly regret not insisting on a pre-publishing proofread by me before it went to press. That local newspaper article didn't stay local; it went out through the whole entire United States through the Associated Press.

You can read the article Bernice refers to here: https://newspaperarchive.com/lincoln-journal-jul-02-1977-p-2/

Before I knew it, my phone rang and a strange voice questioned me as to whether I had ever lived in California and if I had ever gone to a school that Graham attended in Los Angeles. That voice reminded me of my schoolgirl chum Ruth

Kendra Blevins Ford

Walker. We went to the same school back in 1907. Sure enough, it was Ruth on the line! We had lost track of each other when she and I married our husbands and took different paths in life. She was calling from Kansas City, Missouri, and had seen the article that was written about me in the local paper. She also said that she would have known me from the picture alone if I had walked down her street that same day, that I looked just like she had remembered. I was amazed and delighted to hear her voice and reconnect with her!

Then I received a call from Ventura from another fine friend who had married, moved on, and due to the change of our last names had lost track of one another. The phone calls were an unexpected "benefit" of the publishing of that article. I also received dozens and dozens of letters; in fact, I received a letter from almost every state in the union with Alaska and Honolulu being the most distant ones. It was a very exciting time, most definitely.

I was utterly shocked that a local newspaper woman would have the audacity to not write up the story as I had told it to her. She chose to use very poor judgment in word choice by calling me a "pin-up girl." Now, the Webster's New World Dictionary's definition for that is, and I quote, "decimating a girl whose sexual attractiveness makes her a subject for the kind of pictures often pinned up on walls."

It's important to note here that this definition has changed over the years and the most recent online definition can be found here: https://www.merriam-webster.com/dictionary/pinup%20girl Bernice would be glad to know that the definition no longer has the sexual connotation it once held, which was rather distressing to her.

I've been pestered almost to distraction over the years by people asking where I posed for the poster, how did it happen, and how much money I received from it. I will say it again for the record, it was purely coincidental that Howard Chandler Christy was at the Navy recruiting office on the exact day and the exact time that I was there. I went to the Navy recruiting office with *one mission*: to enlist, and enlist I did!

Then a former neighbor of mine happened to call me, who lived in Port Angeles, who was a former captain in the Navy and knew Harry, my former husband and Graham's father. Ironically he didn't know that women had served in the First World War! He told some Navy friends of his, and a certain Chief Warrant Officer was a very good friend of his and a friend of mine.

Kendra Blevins Ford

This particular Chief Warrant Officer happened to call me and was surprised to learn that women had indeed served in the Navy. He determined that some acknowledgment of women who served in the Navy was due. He knew of so many admirals by the first name that he was able to accomplish something I had never dreamed of. He was able to obtain permission for the U.S.S. Orleck to come over to Port Angeles from Tacoma. They had invited me on board for a special dinner.

At precisely 4:30 p.m., December 17, 1977, I was escorted between a guard of honor by Captain Martin Sibitsky and Lieutenant Fred Feakes. And piped aboard the ship, I was welcomed by Commander Robert Sheridan, and Executive Officer Lee Doolittle, USN. In case you do not know what I mean by "piped aboard," in this case, four chief boatswain's mates are lined up next to the gangplank. As soon as I reached the gangplank, they blew a long blast on their whistles until I was on board ship.

They Said She Couldn't So She Did

This was a rare honor, actually—especially since I was a woman, of only a Chief Yeoman (F) rating. This recognition would in most cases be reserved only for heads of countries, perhaps a widow of one of our presidents, or even an admiral.

Kendra Blevins Ford

We went into the officer's mess hall and I was given the opportunity to autograph used naval recruitment posters. I was given a beautiful bouquet of American beauty roses, and a plaque with the emblem of the U.S.S. Orleck, DD-886 on it. We had a most delicious dinner and visited for a while. At the end of the evening, I was taken down by Lieutenant Feakes, who also escorted me home. This, by far, was the most thrilling experience of my entire life and I shall never, ever forget it.

The city of Sequim had advanced by leaps and bounds, which was perplexing to some people. They would have liked Sequim to remain quaint and charming, but even the cutest baby reaches a time when it's all arms and legs, and trips over its own feet. Very few streets were paved in Sequim at this writing, and still fewer streets had sidewalks to walk on here. The main street through town was also known as Highway 101, and the car traffic was increasing every year. Most of the population seemed to be mature adults, some more mature than others! Several women I knew still rode their bicycles to go shopping or to visit the post office or library.

When I first came to Sequim, I had trouble walking as much or as frequently as I had been accustomed to. Ever since I had that stroke when I was at Ballard, my right foot turned into

They Said She Couldn't So She Did

my left one and I had to be very careful not to trip over it. I also suffered from constant pain in my right hip. Someone suggested that I see a local masseur, here in town, and see if he could do something about the chronic pain in my hip, so I did, figuring I had nothing to lose. Well, I went to see this person and this is what he did: he suddenly grabbed my right foot and jerked it, like pulled it forward. That was all. I had about eight blocks to walk back home and I absolutely dreaded getting up and down those curbs. The first curb, I just stepped down like anyone else, and lo and behold, my foot was in the proper position! And it didn't hurt a bit when I put my weight on it! My, what a relief it was to walk normally again. I could now take long walks around the neighborhood and actually enjoy it!

Well, as luck would have it, I was crossing the main highway in February of 1978, and the traffic signal said "go" and so I proceeded to cross the street. I was about halfway across the street when a small truck jumped the traffic signal and headed straight for me. Surprise and alarm overtook my instincts and I tried to take two quick steps to avoid being hit, but tripped over my own feet and fell flat on my face in front of the truck! The driver of the truck saw me and stopped suddenly. He said he didn't see me in the street until I fell. He was so close to hitting me, he couldn't stand between the bumper of his truck and where my body lay in the street or his truck would have driven over me. That is just too doggone close in my opinion! The young man truly felt bad, took the blame for it, and insisted that I go to the doctor to get checked over. The policeman escorted me to the hospital, but the young man paid my bill for it.

A few weeks later, I felt a pain in my side and went back to the doctor to investigate the cause. In the emergency room, he had x-rayed my *ankle* when I said it was my *knee* that hurt after the accident. This time he didn't even x-ray me, but instead put a "rib cage" on over my chest and said, "Well, you may have fractured a rib." Well, I found that the rib cage actually helped. Then, several weeks later, my left knee was still very painful for me. I went to another doctor and his x-ray showed that I had chipped my knee cap when I fell. This doctor was able to fix up my knee and get it back to normal; I was even able to enjoy walking again. How silly that it took this many doctor visits just to figure out what all my injuries were from the one accident.

There was a very nice transportation system program that was developed in the town of Sequim. It was called "Wheels." Some people volunteered to drive senior citizens to places too far for them to walk to, such as a doctor's appointment when you are ill, to the grocery or other shopping, or even the new nutrition center. We could buy a book of ten tickets for just a dollar. You gave one ticket to the driver each way, which amounted to only ten cents each way! It was a very nice service in of itself, but especially in the rain, snow, or windy weather. The program was financed by the county and the drivers got paid a dollar per trip, plus 15 cents per mile.

The nutrition center was also for senior citizens. One meal per day was available to senior citizens, who were served at 4:30 p.m., and cost just one dollar. For this meal, we were served fruit juice, salad, two vegetables, the main dish meat, plus milk, tea, buttermilk or coffee, and of course, a dessert. If one was too ill to go there, then the meal could be arranged to be brought to them. The manager of this nutrition center was a very good cook, a chef even. He knew how to roast meat properly and not dry it out. One particular salad that everyone enjoyed had sliced sweet onions, sliced cooked carrots, and green pepper that is marinated in a sweet and sour spiced dressing. Although they did not serve meals on Saturday or Sunday in person, they ensured that their customers ate by sending out frozen meals to their homes instead.

I bought a lovely wheelchair that I use like a walker. I could walk three miles per day, three days per week with it, usually to the grocery store or to the library. One day I had walked down to the grocery store (and it was the first warm day of the year) and I was getting rather tired, so I decided to stop and rest under the shade of a large tree. I was minding my own business and eating a banana when a car came rushing up the highway, slammed on its brakes right opposite of me, and two people jumped out of the car and rushed over to me. I didn't recognize them at first. They said, "Bernice, are you alright!?" Confused, I looked at them quizzically and said, "Yes, I'm just sitting here resting." The couple responded by saying, "Well, we had never seen you actually sit in that wheelchair. We were afraid that something had happened to you, and so we were going to take you back home." The man in this couple was quite the jokester, and he waggled his finger in front of my face and said, "Now see here, ma'am, when you live in Washington, you eat apples; you don't eat bananas!" Well, we both had quite a good laugh from that comment.

When I lived in Sequim, I had, by the help of the public library, been getting large print books to read. The library of Congress in Washington D.C. also supplied a free machine on which you could play "talking books." This was a great blessing to me especially because I had recently learned around that time that my vision was only 200/20 in each eye, making me legally

They Said She Couldn't So She Did

blind. I was also having considerable discomfort in breathing with no apparent reason for it. I felt the atmosphere was not right for my breathing, so I moved to Shelton, where it would be easier to reach Graham if I needed him urgently.

Chapter 19

Shelton

My cost of living was out of control. Gasoline was a whopping $1.25 a gallon in some places, perhaps even higher in others. It was about a two-hour drive from Lake Cushman, where my son Graham lived, to Sequim. With gasoline that high, and no sign of it going down, it seemed advisable to find a new place near Graham.

Graham had retired from the insurance business, so he now had a place to call home permanently. They lived aboard their yacht for several years and then lived in a motor home. This was very necessary because of his traveling about 1,000 miles per month for the insurance company he worked for. The boat and motor home were places to eat and sleep mainly and to go here and there in, but not truly a home. He lived in the kitchen and the bathroom in the cabin at the lake, which was another place to sleep and eat in. They have good comfortable furniture and a real honest-to-goodness permanent home atmosphere at last.

They Said She Couldn't So She Did

Naturally, in an apartment, one doesn't enjoy smelling the same thing everyone else is cooking. Now, however, people have microwaves where you can cook in seconds and have no lingering food smell. It seems like forever long since I've smelled coffee and bacon cooking. When I worked at Gall's we spent a lot of money to make ourselves smell nice, I believe they say to "smell pretty." That's another thing: you smell with your nose, you see with your eyes, you do not see with your nose or smell with your eyes, so why say "you smell pretty" unless you are behind them? That is a different matter! I'll let you think about that for a moment. You do use your sense of smell to guide you if you are blind, however. Given my vision challenges, I began using my sense of smell more acutely then I did my vision.

Let me take a moment to talk about the world we live in. Teenagers are committing suicide and people wonder why. The world is not giving them *anything* really worthwhile to look forward to. For entertainment, you can listen to people being shot to death, watch people get disgustingly drunk, talk about war bombs, and listen to drums and cymbals. To top it all off, an astonishing number of little children and teenagers are losing their hearing because of loud noises in movies, loud music, and the like.

Kendra Blevins Ford

Shelton was a place for senior citizens like me to live in. The accommodations included one room and your own bath, three square meals a day, and you could even have your own furniture in your room (and I thank God for that!)

I had a beautifully rich, mellow-toned Hammond spinet organ I taught myself to play. I was thankful that I was able to bring my organ to the senior living housing I secured in Shelton. One day I went to the room where my little organ is and put the vital pedal clear down, then truly "soft-pedaled it" and in no time, I could hear the harmony of some little songs. Of course, others heard me play and so I told them, "Tell me what you like, and I'll try to play it. If I cannot, I'll make a note of it and learn to play it. I cannot play and sing at the same time, so you folks will have to do your share." We sang for an hour together, mistakes and all. One old gentleman became so relaxed, he took a nap while we played and sang. Our kind of music didn't disturb him at all.

Early one morning I was lying in my bed when all of a sudden, I heard two men in my room saying, "Get up, get up, we have a fire!" Well, believe you me, that will wake you up, wide awake, faster than any other method known to man. The two strangers were firemen; they urgently pulled me up into a sitting position, one quickly put on my slippers, the other wasted no time plunging my arms into my bathrobe, then both of them all but thrust me into my wheelchair. During our rapid exit, I snatched a blanket off my bed, wrapped it around my shoulders, and I must say in retrospect, this was all done in one fluid motion. As I passed the clothes closet door, I snatched my other robe. When we opened the door, that awful acrid smell of smoke must have given wings to our feet. The firemen rushed to the stairway, lifted up my wheelchair as if it had wings and carried me downstairs, out the front door and across the street. The street was littered with fire engines, ambulances, policeman, everybody helping, with surprisingly zero panic, with no screams for help. Over 50 elderly people living in my building were accounted for in under five minutes. Now that's an absolute miracle that literally unfolded right in front of their eyes, and we thanked God for it.

We were rushed across the street to the Pine Street Inn and quick as a wink, someone asked, "Would you like a cup of hot coffee or some fruit juice?" That was two o'clock in the morning! But truly, everyone was so kind to us. In a few minutes, we were all loaded onto an ambulance and whisked off to the hospital to be evaluated. There, we were asked for our personal information and then hospital identification bracelets were placed on our wrists. We were asked about whom to contact for next of kin. I had Graham's phone number on a card in my purse, but not my grandson James. I knew he would know Graham would not be home, as he was most likely in Port Angeles or Victoria. I had not been smart enough to write his motor vehicle license plate number down so that he could be located by law enforcement swiftly. I was getting awfully tired, and then it came to me: Graham had said that James was going to be at the lake! But unfortunately, he wasn't. Of course, I was a little worried as to where I should go, as others had relatives within easy phoning distance but mine could not be reached. One by one, my neighbors were being taken to some alternative place to stay, until we could all return to our apartments. About 3:45 a.m., the nurse came over and said that someone from one of the churches was on her way to pick me up and keep me as long as necessary. Mrs. Roger Conley came over to me and said, "My name is Vickie. Bernice, we want you to stay with us until you can go back to your apartment." We tip-toed into her home and didn't wake anyone up except for a little roly-poly dog and Doty, a Siamese cat. Doty and I assumed mutual comfort with one another and I fell asleep before she stopped purring. Vickie left a small light burning in the bathroom for me. I woke up about my usual time, slipped quietly into the bathroom. I had

They Said She Couldn't So She Did

just turned open the doorknob when a small, toothless, big-eyed little boy said, "Who's you?" Poor little boy, he seemed scared of me! I gently told him that his mama had brought me home to stay for a few days and to be real quiet so she could go back to sleep. I whispered slowly to him, "You go back to bed and I'll go back to bed, too. Here, I'll show you where I'm sleeping; see how Doty is sleeping with me, too. Is that okay?" He nodded emphatically and toddled back to his bed.

Many of us couldn't return to our apartments until Saturday. Some of the residents of my building could not return for some time after that. On the west side of our building, some of our windows were broken due to the heat. The fire had originated in the hardware store, the third building down the street from us. The paint and ammunition housed within the building had exploded and spread the fire rather quickly. The hardware store was a total loss, as was the flower shop next door. Keeping water on our building ultimately saved it, but the water and smoke were not easily nor quickly disposed of. As people had been shooting off firecrackers from about nine o'clock to midnight the night of the fire, I suspect one of the errant firecrackers was to blame. I recall turning over on my good hearing ear so I could go to sleep the night of the fire.

Kendra Blevins Ford

After my rescue, when we were downstairs, I was amazed at the noise: firemen giving directions by bullhorn and fire truck engines running to pump water. I guess I am getting used to the neighborhood noise (thanks to the cruising of the younger generation), but I just couldn't turn the firecracker noise off. Anyway, I'm home safe and sound. Even though you may be reading this years later, please thank God for our safety.

Chapter 20

Washington Veterans Home

While living in Sequim, I often had spells of shortness of breath, and my vision was less and less reliable. The daily medication became necessary for me. And a lack of immediate help, medically speaking, was proving to be a concern. I felt a veteran's home was my only solution at that point given my advanced age. Moving to such a facility meant that medical staff would be available as needed, my meals would be taken care of, and I would live with people within my own age bracket. And so, yet again, I moved, not knowing at the time that this would indeed be my final home.

I distributed more of my personal things, including my beloved little organ which I bought in Sequim. So here I am, in the Washington Veteran's Home, in Retsil, Washington. I have had cataracts removed from both eyes now and the recovery was incredibly slow and not nearly as satisfactory as I had been led to expect. I realized then that I would just have to accept my vision the way that it was, as well as the physical limitations I was beginning to feel in my body as time marched on.

I have a lovely room at the veteran's home and share it with one other lady person, while we share a bathroom with one other lady, too. My room looks out on to the bay, and I can see the Navy shipyard, which is about nine miles by car around the bay. The bay is surrounded by hills of various heights and colored with trees. To my right, as far as I can see, is, some say, Mt. Baker; others say it is Mt. Rainier. It's still a beautiful view regardless of its name. To my left, is the area where my son Graham lives. The grounds are well landscaped here and are beautiful to behold. There's a very long unusual looking building with a turret. There is the main mess hall, a library, and an auditorium, where they have a lovely Hammond organ. As you may guess, I am not in my room all of the time, but here is a clue where I just may be!

The doctor I was sent over to see regarding the numbness in my right hand, is running a research study of older people in their 80s who were premature babies, weighing four pounds or less at birth, and are currently having poor circulation or arthritis. His theory was this: could our main arteries been less than fully developed at birth because of our low birth weight. My weight at birth was 14 ounces, and that astonished him! They forbid me to exercise as it could stimulate too much circulation that could potentially cause a blood clot. Medication in the form of a nitroglycerine patch was prescribed for me that was applied both day and night, half an inch of the stuff was squeezed out of a tube (like a toothpaste) on to a measuring piece of paper. This was taped onto one of my shoulder blades every morning, and then the opposite one in the evening. After five months, a new system was tried. A circular pad with the same medication was applied like a Band-Aid, every night, with no further morning applications. It made me light-headed at first, but I'm okay now. They sent me to another specialist to evaluate the hand numbness, and at this writing they are still waiting on the final report. I'm not allowed to go outdoors in fog, wind, rain, or cold weather as that makes me quite short of breath, and oxygen is paramount to breathing. The doctors deliberate back and forth regarding the idea of operating in order to flush my large arteries. They are concerned that if they don't operate, I could have yet another serious stroke. I wonder what medical science will have learned from my particular medical case years from now when I am long gone.

Kendra Blevins Ford

I was quite fascinated by this research revelation, as I have worked many years as a clinical research nurse. I was rather astounded to learn that my great-grandmother's birth weight was less than a pound at birth, and that was back in 1897! No wonder she states that she was a "sickly child" for most of her childhood. She definitely had a disadvantage in being so tiny at birth. I attempted to find her birth certificate, but was unsuccessful. It seems that the further back in time you search, the more difficult it is to find documentation for important events. So while this extremely low birth weight information she reports may be more fable than fact, it is from my great-grandmother's lips, and I'll just leave it at that.

While I was living at the Washington Veteran's Home, there was a Civil War veteran who was 104 years old with his 97-year-old wife living here by his side at the home. He was one of the people who thoroughly enjoyed my organ playing. I fondly recall that he enjoyed listening to my playing "Lolita" and "Beautiful Dreamer" when they requested it. We all enjoyed the soft slow music that we grew up with. This long-lived couple passed away just a month apart from each other, almost to the day. What a long and beautiful relationship they must have shared together.

As far as I am concerned, the Washington Veteran's Home has pulled out all of the stops in regards to entertainment

They Said She Couldn't So She Did

for us. There is far too much happening; they want you on the go, all of the time. The music they play for us is much too loud, and entirely too fast. At our advanced ages, we are not able to go, go, go! They greatly overdo refreshments here. Imagine this: ice cream cones at 11 a.m. and the main midday meal at 11:30. A sundae special at 4 p.m., supper at 5, with a special treat that included cake or cookies, ice cream, and coffee. And we wonder why so many people are overweight.

Graham planned a most delightful Mother's Day for me one year. He asked all of my grandchildren and their families to come to a resort with cabins on the lake where we could all spend the weekend together. Paul and family from Chicago, James and family from Denver, Helene and her husband Rick from California, Cindy and family, and also Rob (who happens to live nearby in Washington). What a lovely idea, I thought. I can see all of them, some of which I haven't seen for years. Helene and Rick had planned to fly up from L.A. to Seattle aboard a seaplane, with plans to land right in front of our cabin! What an incredible way to to arrive at our gathering. Donnie and Graham came to pick me up about 9:00 a.m. so that we can get to the resort in time to see them step off of the plane. Well, imagine our surprise when Helene didn't arrive by the highly anticipated plane. So Graham went over to the reception desk to see when they would arrive and then saw Helene and Rick in the lobby! By the way, Helene and Rick had just celebrated their first wedding anniversary at the time of this gathering. The cabin was furnished well and included dishes, a stove and refrigerator, enabling us to cook and eat in the cabin. Unfortunately, that meant a lot of work for Donnie, but she thrives on spur-of-the-moment cooking, I think. Cindy brought a lovely cake, which was the most beautifully decorated cake I had ever seen. She also was the one who baked the cake, as she is a professional at this and even teaches it. Her two youngsters are the best-behaved children I've seen in a long time, they were a joy to be around. Paul and his family were unable to attend, nor could James and his family. Previously scheduled graduation festivities made it time and cost prohibitive for them, unfortunately.

I have found that my body does not adjust to sudden changes as quickly as it used to. I asked Graham and Donnie to take me home on a Monday, which was sooner than we had originally planned. Graham, Donnie, and I had a lovely lunch downtown on the last day, and then we said goodbye to Helene and Rick.

Later that day, I had supper at the Washington Veteran's Home at 4:30 as usual. When I came back to my room after

They Said She Couldn't So She Did

supper, I saw a multitude of watercraft: rowboats, motorboats, even sailboats dotted all over the bay, making it look like someone had upset a popcorn machine! I have never seen quite so many ships in one place. I counted 121 of them! I heard an airplane overhead and saw it descend *extremely* low, so much so that I thought it was going to crash land in the Navy yard. Faster than I can write it, planes came over, flew around the bend, so I quickly grabbed my opera glasses and looked as far as I could see, and sure enough, at the point where the ferry comes around the bend, I saw a dark gray object. I saw what appeared to be a Coast Guard vessel hurrying toward the large object to keep small watercraft from getting too close to it. Finally, my view improved and I could see her distinctly, for she was huge! I had never seen such a large aircraft carrier.

The flight deck was covered with private cars of families that will live here while she was in dry dock. All of the yacht clubs hereabouts were decked out to escort the new USS Ranger to the Navy yard. They were quite close. Fireboats were putting up a grand display, with fireworks being set off as a salute; all small watercraft and cars along the shoreline were sounding their horns simultaneously. I heard that she had returned from Lebanon and Mediterranean duty. I never saw such a sight! And what a surprise to get home in time to observe the grand display.

Helene and Rick later informed me that they saw this all from the air as their plane happened to fly over at just the right moment.

May 14, 1984, is another day not soon to be forgotten. It was a farewell to the Mighty Mo. She was leaving for Long Beach Naval Shipyard. Just the reverse, only a bigger send off than the welcoming home of the USS Ranger. The Mighty Mo was commissioned in 1944, served in Iwo Jima, as well as Okinawa, Tokyo, and it was on the USS Missouri that the Japanese signed the surrender papers on September 2, 1945. The Mighty Mo arrived in Bremerton in 1954. She was to be deactivated in Long Beach.

They Said She Couldn't So She Did

Today is a good day, and I feel okay, like the person I was just a couple of years ago. Remember how I said at the beginning that I have lived in a most amazing age? I still believe that to be true about my life. I am delighted to learn that I will become a great-grandmother again, in about nine months. I have to ask Helene and Rick for more information on this.

Based on this statement, this recording was completed sometime in 1984 as the baby-to-be that Bernice is referring to here is Andrea Swartz, born in 1985. The picture above was taken in 1988, just two years before she passed away and the very last time I saw her. From left to right: Kendra Blevins Ford, Bernice Smith Blevins Tongate, and Andrea Swartz Stafl.

Kendra Blevins Ford

Bernice finishes her audio recordings by saying,

So long, my dears. I hope this will be interesting for you. I love you all *very much*.

The end of Bernice's story, and her final words, spoken by her, caused me to feel sad as if I had to say goodbye to her all over again. Listening to the words of her story allowed me to get to know the person I really never knew well at all. My wish to you, the reader, is that you cherish your elders while you still can. They hold a lifetime of wisdom we all may benefit from. I am most proud of this strong American woman, a part of my history, as well as my family. May she forever rest in peace.

Acknowledgements

There are several people who were instrumental in bringing this idea, this dream, a reality. My sincerest thanks goes to my parents, Paul and Kathy Blevins, for encouraging me to do this, to listen to the words, write the story, and let my great-grandmother's voice be heard. Thanks also to my aunt, Helene Hall, and my uncle, James Blevins, who were gracious to send me memorabilia that were a part of Bernice's estate, Graham Blevins' estate, and even Harrison Blevins' estate. The photos selected for this work are, in my opinion, treasured heirlooms which enhance Bernice's life story as only pictures can. Thanks also goes to my editor, Mary Carver, who provided valuable editing, proofreading, and perspective. And a big thanks to Michelle Morrow for her expertise in formatting my book, she added the final polish I was longing for. And finally, thanks to my husband, Chris Ford, for his undying support throughout the many hours I spent on this project.

For Further Reading

National WWI History Museum

https://theworldwar.pastperfectonline.com/byperson?keyword=Smith%20Tongate,%20Bernice

Bernice's Grave Marker

https://www.findagrave.com/memorial/37479445/bernice-tongate

Petticoats in the Navy

https://www.cooperhewitt.org/2013/09/06/petticoats-in-the-navy/

Associated Press Article 1985

https://www.apnews.com/0c9ac862ae0bfb9cc4fbb08573c8dc28

U.S. Dept. of Defense

http://archive.defense.gov/news/newsarticle.aspx?id=42931

Newspaper Article: U.S. Navy's First Pin-Up Girl is Now 80

They Said She Couldn't So She Did

https://newspaperarchive.com/lincoln-journal-jul-02-1977-p-2/

Obituary in Washington Post

https://www.washingtonpost.com/archive/local/1990/01/27/deaths/7c7101b7-d7ff-4754-b3e0-1e388293ed50/?utm_term=.6b1e1dcca246

American Battle Monuments Commission article

https://www.abmc.gov/news-events/news/womens-history-month-navy-yeoman-world-war-1

Photo of Bernice from American Women in World War I

https://books.google.com/books?id=Yr69AwAAQBAJ&pg=PT30&lpg=PT30&dq=bernice+smith+tongate&source=bl&ots=TnjUfA536L&sig=ACfU3U1bjgaF3YRz7ZF4vKORD1cWjLTUTw&hl=en&sa=X&ved=2ahUKEwiq1M2fn5LhAhUm3YMKHWt4ApEQ6AEwD3oECAgQAQ#v=onepage&q=bernice%20smith%20tongate&f=false

Excerpt from the Healy Lectures 2005-2015 (page 119)

https://books.google.com/books?id=ozMrDwAAQBAJ&pg=PA119&lpg=PA119&dq=bernice+smith+tongate&source=bl&ots=dpDV_kAXeC&sig=ACfU3U3P7jn9237xd2kcPLkVyHtT55jjIg&hl=en&sa=X&ved=2ahUKEwiq1M2fn5LhAhUm

3YMKHWt4ApEQ6AEwEHoECAcQAQ#v=onepage&q=bernice%20smith%20tongate&f=false

Seattle Times Obituary

http://community.seattletimes.nwsource.com/archive/?date=19900126&slug=1052826

Deskgram.com #Yeomanette posts

https://deskgram.net/explore/tags/yeomanette

Social Media Recognition

https://www.facebook.com/notes/puget-sound-navy-museum/puget-sound-navy-museum-image-of-the-week/198398073511671/

Grave Marker of Bernice's 1st Husband Harry

https://www.findagrave.com/memorial/85350906/harrison-halstead-blevins

Pritzker Military Museum and Library

https://www.pritzkermilitary.org/explore/museum/past-exhibits/american-icons-great-war/gee-i-wish-i-were-man/

Pritzker Military Museum and Library

American Icons of the Great War: Christy Girl

They Said She Couldn't So She Did

https://www.pritzkermilitary.org/explore/museum/past-exhibits/american-icons-great-war/christy-girl/

Women and War

http://www.stlawu.edu/gallery/education/f/gs103-3-10-4.php

In the Library of Congress

https://www.loc.gov/pictures/item/2002712088/

Englewood Review Article

https://englewoodreview.com/main.asp?SectionID=10&SubSectionID=15&ArticleID=302&TM=17708

New York Historical Society Museum and Library

http://behindthescenes.nyhistory.org/depiction-women-propaganda-posters/

Map of Alaska

https://www.travelalaska.com/Destinations/Communities/Kotzebue.aspx

From Fish to Candle

https://video.nationalgeographic.com/video/news/0000014e-7891-deef-a9ee-7abf4e1a0000

Kendra Blevins Ford

USS Orleck DD-886

http://www.hnsa.org/hnsa-ships/uss-orleck-dd-886/

https://newspaperarchive.com/lincoln-journal-jul-02-1977-p-2/

Contact Kendra Blevins Ford

Via Facebook Page:

https://www.facebook.com/theysaidshecouldntsoshedid/

Via Goodreads:

https://www.goodreads.com/user/show/75743728-kendra

Made in the USA
Columbia, SC
03 November 2019